CHEKHOV IN MY LIFE

LYDIA AVILOVA

Chekhov in My Life
A Love Story

Translated with an Introduction by
DAVID MAGARSHACK

With drawings by
LYNTON LAMB

METHUEN DRAMA

First published in 1950 by John Lehmann Limited.
This new edition with additional material first published in 1989
by Methuen Drama, Michelin House, 81 Fulham Road, London SW3 6RB
and distributed in the United States of America by
HEB Inc., 70 Court Street, Portsmouth, New Hampshire 03801

British Library Cataloguing in Publication Data

Avilova, Lydia
Chekhov in my life.
1. Drama in Russian. Chekhov, A. P. (Anton Pavlovich),
1860–1904
I. Title
891.72'3

ISBN 0-413-62120-0

Printed in Great Britain by
St Edmundsbury Press Limited, Bury St Edmunds, Suffolk

*Lynton Lamb's drawing on the title
page was adapted from a portrait of
Chekhov as a student, painted in 1880
by his brother, N. P. Chekhov*

PREFACE TO THE NEW EDITION

Chekhov and Lydia Avilova

IN THE tenth volume of the complete edition of his works, published in 1935, Ivan Bunin, a close friend of Chekhov and Lydia Avilova, wrote: "Was there at least one great love in Chekhov's life? I don't think there was." In 1953 Bunin underlined these lines in red pencil and wrote "in a firm hand," according to his wife, "Yes, there was. With Lydia Avilova."

"I knew Lydia Avilova very well," Bunin wrote in his unfinished manuscript *About Chekhov*, "and the distinguishing traits of her character were truthfulness, intelligence, talent, modesty, a rare sense of humour even if directed against herself. After reading her reminiscences I got a different idea of Chekhov and I saw him in quite a new light. I never suspected the relationship that existed between them. Yet people still think that Chekhov never experienced a great love. I had thought so myself, but now I can say emphatically: he did experience such a love—for Lydia Avilova.

"I cannot help feeling that some people may ask: can one have absolute trust in her reminiscences? Lydia Avilova was quite exceptionally truthful. She did not conceal even the critical remarks Chekhov made about her writings nor what he had said about her. She never hinted at her love for Chekhov during her lifetime (and I had met her frequently). And yet to think how many years she had concealed it. A rare woman!

"I read the introduction to her reminiscences by a certain Kotov and I was amazed at his stupidity. He writes: 'For all that one cannot conceal the extraordinary subjectivity and onesidedness of the author [Lydia Avilova] in her treatment of the material in connection with Chekhov. One can hardly consider it entirely credible that Chekhov

had expressed his feelings for Lydia Avilova in his story *About Love*.*
Actually, Chekhov's attitude towards Lydia Avilova is revealed in his
interest in her as a writer who could have dealt with the highly
relevant subject of a woman's dependent position and the abnormali-
ties of family life.'"

Ivan Bunin underlined the last sentence and wrote in the margin in
blue pencil: "What an extraordinary * * * to have written that!"

That Bunin never changed his mind about the real relationship
between Chekhov and Lydia Avilova is clear from a letter I received
from Mrs. Bunin on February 9, 1956. "I know," she wrote, "that your
opinion (about the love affair of Chekhov with Lydia Avilova)
coincided with the opinion of my late husband."

The eloquent asterisks with which Bunin expressed his opinion of
Kotov could be quite legitimately applied to Professor Ernest J.
Simmons' laborious attempt to discredit Lydia Avilova's reminiscences published under the title *Chekhov in My Life*. A quotation or two
should suffice to show how utterly divorced from life the mind of an
academic can be. Professor Simmons writes: "Yet it is certainly a
curious fact that though Bunin and Lydia Avilova were devoted
admirers of Chekhov, not one word about him appears in their
letters." Is it so curious? Would not the very fact of their "great love"
have precluded Lydia from mentioning Chekhov in her letters or,
indeed, as Bunin himself implies, in her talks with Bunin? To quote
Professor Simmons again: "That Chekhov's exaggerated sense of
duty to his family at that time could have prevented him from
confirming a love once conceived is probably true, but it can be just as
logically argued that it would have kept him from falling in love at
all." A logical or ridiculous argument?

Professor Simmons finally quotes Chekhov's sister Masha to clinch
his theory that there was "no tangible evidence" on Chekhov's part
that he was in love with Lydia Avilova. Masha, it seems, declared in
that characteristically proprietorial way of hers that there was "nothing to it" and that it was all "a fantasy." Does anyone really expect
her to have said anything else? Is it not a fact that Chekhov never
discussed his intimate life with her? Is it not also a fact that she was
dead set against Chekhov's marriage to Olga Knipper?

—DAVID MAGARSHACK

* Professor Simmons repeats this statement almost word for word!

INTRODUCTION TO

THE FIRST EDITION

S O MUCH has been written about Chekhov that little of any importance, it would seem, could have escaped his biographers or critics. And yet it is only recently that one of the most significant events of his life has come to light with the publication in Moscow of a volume of personal reminiscences of Chekhov by various hands. This volume contains an account by Lydia Avilova, the wife of a Petersburg official and herself a writer of short stories, describing the unhappy love affair between her and Chekhov which lasted for ten years and covered the most important period of Chekhov's authorship. This hitherto unknown chapter in Chekhov's life certainly seems to explain more than anything else the peculiar " heart-ache " motif that runs through most of his stories and plays, the sadness that, like the mournful sound of the breaking violin string in *The Cherry Orchard*, is so typical of his creative genius and so characteristic a feature of almost every love story in his writings.

Lydia Avilova was four years younger than Chekhov. She was born in Moscow in 1864, and she was only twenty-four when she first met Chekhov. In the account of her relations with Chekhov, published several years after her death in 1942 at the age of seventy-eight under the title of *Chekhov in My Life*, she only describes eight meetings with Chekhov between 1889 and 1899, but it is clear from the text that they must have met much more often. Lydia Avilova's memoirs contain a great deal of highly interesting literary material, but what is

7

particularly important is the biographical data they supply about *The Seagull*, Chekhov's most imaginative play that has exercised the ingenuity of many critics, whose guesses about the origin of many of the characters in the play seem now to have been widely off the mark.

It is certainly a most curious fact that Chekhov, whose short life (he died in 1904 at the age of forty-four) was spent among his family and numerous friends, should still remain the most enigmatic of all great Russian writers. The mystery with which Chekhov surrounded himself becomes even greater when one considers that, unlike most of the great Russian writers and contrary to what is generally believed of him outside Russia, he was essentially a man with a very strongly developed sense of social duty. His journey to the remote Pacific island of Sakhalin for the purpose of studying the conditions of the convict settlements there is well known. His account of it is to be published by the Folio Society in 1990. But what is not so well known and what remained unknown even in Russia during his lifetime is that, in spite of his growing fame as a writer, he engaged in a free medical practice among the villagers near his small country place of Melikhovo and that he took a keen personal interest in the spreading of education among the peasants. The slenderness of his means did not deter him from building a village hospital and three village schools at his own expense, and he was also responsible for the foundation of the public library in his native town of Taganrog which he kept supplied with books to the end of his life. He never spoke or wrote about his numerous social activities, but they certainly belie the general idea of him as a man who was indifferent to the social conditions of his day. Combined with his violent dislike of tendentiousness in literature, this reserve of his helped to produce

the " legend " of a writer who preached the gospel of resigna-
tion, an idea that is still responsible for the widespread
misinterpretation of his works and particularly of his plays.

Chekhov's almost morbid reserve was not due to an
intellectual attitude towards life based on the idea of a passive
acceptance of evil. This peculiar trait of Chekhov's character
seems rather to derive from the days of his early childhood
when he reacted very violently to the harsh treatment meted
out by his father, who was a great believer in the principle
that to spare the rod was to spoil the child. This deep-seated
conflict with his father (a poor shopkeeper, who went bankrupt
when Chekhov was only a boy of fifteen, and had to run away
from his creditors to Moscow where his family lived in dire
penury in a basement until Chekhov began to earn enough
to be able to support it) left an indelible mark on Chekhov's
character. He never liked his father even when he had no
longer any reason to fear him. Their relationship was always
strained, and in a characteristic entry in his diary, the old man
sums it up in three words : " Anton is angry." When one
considers how incongruous this adjective sounds in view of
Chekhov's mild and gentle character, this entry is certainly
significant. But there is more direct evidence of Chekhov's
attitude to his father. Potapenko, a popular second-rate
novelist who was an intimate friend of Chekhov's, contrasts,
in his reminiscences of the great writer, his tender love for
his mother and his aloof and almost stern attitude to his father.
" To his father," he writes, " Chekhov always showed the
respect that is due from a son to a father. But while assuring
him a comfortable old age, Chekhov could never forget his
father's harsh discipline during the days when he was still
the head of the family in Taganrog. Sometimes, pointing to
his father, who had become a quiet, peaceful and friendly old

9

man, Chekhov used to recall how he would force his children to go to church and how if any of his sons (Chekhov was the second of five boys) showed any lack of zeal, he would not hesitate to birch him mercilessly. Chekhov, no doubt, recalled it without any resentment, but there could be no doubt that it had left a deep trace in his soul. He used to say that in those days his father was a cruel man.

"Chekhov could never forgive his father for thrashing him, as even as a child he could not tolerate violence of any sort" Potapenko continues. "He also considered that his father made his early years unhappy by the narrow religious education he gave him which made Chekhov always detest the imposition of religious beliefs. Talking of the methods of a famous Russian pedagogue, Chekhov said to me, 'If his pupils are happy, then they are luckier than my brothers and myself were, for our childhood was a time of great suffering for us.' And though when Chekhov was telling me all this it was ancient history and the old man had long ago ceased to be of any importance in his life, spending his last days in prayer and the reading of sacred books, and pleased with his son's fame, and though Chekhov's attitude towards him had always been friendly and even respectful, never by a single word reminding him of the past, that past had never been forgotten, for it had left too deep a scar on Chekhov's sensitive soul."

Chekhov's retiring disposition no doubt grew stronger as a result of his being left to fend for himself as a boy of fifteen, when his family fled to Moscow and he had to stay behind to finish his studies at the secondary school and qualify for entrance to the medical faculty of Moscow University, which he left in 1884.

This deeply rooted aversion from showing his feelings or revealing his innermost thoughts, except perhaps by a hint or a joke, produced that feeling of loneliness in Chekhov to which he gave outward expression by the seal he wore on his watch-chain with the inscription, "To the lonely the world's a desert," with which he sealed some of his letters to Lydia Avilov. Taken together with his hyper-sensitiveness to the feelings of other people and his fear of hurting them or doing anything that might compromise them, it goes a long way to explain the fact that his own feelings for Lydia Avilova escaped the notice of most of his friends and came to light only recently.

Chekhov first met Lydia Avilova only a few years after he was beginning to be talked of as a future great writer. The actual meeting took place on 24th January 1889, at the house of Lydia's brother-in-law, Sergey Khudekov, the owner and editor of *The Petersburg Gazette*, to which Chekhov had been a regular contributor between 1885 and 1888. Chekhov, who was then twenty-nine years old, had already published three volumes of short stories, including some of his most famous ones, such as *The Steppe*, though mostly of a light, humorous nature. About that time he met the well-known Russian writer Vladimir Korolenko, who left this description of him : " I saw before me a young man who looked even younger than his actual age. He was just over medium height, with an oblong, regular, clean-cut face which had not yet lost its characteristic youthful contours. His face, indeed, had something peculiar about it which I could not define at once and which my wife, who had also met Chekhov, afterwards defined as a face which, though undoubtedly that of an educated man, possessed something which reminded her of a village lad. And that was particularly attractive. Even Chekhov's eyes, blue, radiant, and deep, were at one and the same time thoughtful and almost childishly artless. The simplicity of his behaviour and speech was the most characteristic part of his personality, as, indeed, it is of his writings too. In general, at my first meeting with him, Chekhov produced the impression of a man who was full of the joy of life. His eyes seemed to irradiate an inexhaustible fund of wit and high spirits, of which his stories were full. But at the same time one also caught in them a glimpse of something that was more profound and that still had to develop. The general impression I got was that of a man who possessed a great deal of irresistible charm."

Chekhov was hardly the sort of man who would allow his fame to go to his head, but at first he seemed least of all impressed by it. " If I possess a gift that is worthy of respect," he wrote to the Russian writer Grigorovich, " then I'm afraid I must confess that so far I have failed to show any respect for it. I am aware that I possess it, but I have never regarded it as of any great value. . . . My family has never thought much of my literary work and they keep telling me not to sacrifice my real profession to my scribbling. I have hundreds of friends in Moscow, and about a dozen writers among them, but I cannot recall a single one who either read anything I wrote or looked upon me as an artist. In Moscow we have a so-called ' literary circle '. If I were to go there and read them even a few lines from your letter, they would laugh in my face. During the five years I have been contributing to all sorts of papers, I have become so used to this general view of my literary insignificance that I cannot help regarding my work with condescension, but—I go on writing. . . . Up to now my literary work has, I'm afraid, been rather thoughtless, careless, and perfunctory. I cannot remember one story on which I spent more than a day, and *Gamekeeper* which you seem to like so much I wrote in the dressing-box of an open-air swimming-bath."

But by the time Chekhov met Lydia Avilova his happy-go-lucky attitude towards literature had undergone a cardinal change. He became fully conscious of his responsibility as a writer and spent much longer over his stories. While in 1886, for instance, Chekhov had published one hundred and fifteen short stories, he published only sixty-five in 1887, and only thirteen in 1888, and that in spite of the fact that in the last two years he devoted less and less time to his medical practice. In 1889 his contributions to the two popular Petersburg journals, *The Petersburg Gazette* and the humorous weekly *Fragments*, edited by Nicholas Leykin, had stopped. The humorous sketch based on some amusing anecdote or some chance encounter, which had formed so large a part of his literary output (*The Daughter of Albion*, for instance, was an English governess, a certain Miss Matthews, he had met while staying in the country with some friends), now gave place to a much deeper observation of life and men and soon led him to adopt a formula for creative work very similar to Wordsworth's famous " emotion recollected in tranquillity ".

" I can only write from memory," he declared many years afterwards, " and not directly from nature. The subject of my story must first go through the filter of my mind, so that only what is typical and important remains in it."

One result of this newly acquired sense of responsibility towards his literary work was Chekhov's eagerness to help all sorts of budding authors who sent him their manuscripts for correction and advice. He stuck to this practice all through his life.

Between his first meeting with Lydia Avilova at the beginning of 1889 and his second meeting with her three years later, Chekhov had settled in the country on his small estate of Melikhovo, where he built himself a little two-roomed hut to which he would retire to do his writing when, as was usual, his house was invaded by visitors ; he had also undertaken his famous journey to the Far East to study the convict settlements on Sakhalin Island, and had made his first journey abroad to Italy and France. His health was already troubling him, and though as a doctor he should have known all the symptoms of consumption, he would not for a long time admit to himself the real nature of his illness.

In January 1892 he met Lydia Avilova for the second time, and this meeting ended disastrously. Lydia's husband (she was already married and the mother of a nine-months-old boy when she met Chekhov for the first time) learned all about Chekhov and his wife from a scurrilous story made up by a writer who had good reason to be jealous of Chekhov's fame. Henceforth Chekhov took particular care to shield Lydia from anything that might give rise to the merest breath of scandal. Chekhov, incidentally, seemed to have had a sort of presentiment that he was destined to be involved in an unhappy love affair, for in a letter to the Petersburg writer and newspaper owner Suvorin a short time before his first meeting with Lydia, he added this curiously prophetic note after complaining of his life in Moscow : " All I want now is an unhappy love affair."

Two more meetings with Lydia followed, the second of these, on 14th February 1895, ending in the tragi-comedy so beautifully described by Lydia in her memoirs. Then immediately after the second meeting followed an event of some literary importance. Lydia, realising that she was as deeply in love with Chekhov as Chekhov was with her, decided to burn her boats and, though by that time a mother of three children of whom she was inordinately fond, sacrifice her family happiness by telling Chekhov that she was ready to leave her husband if he wanted her to. She chose a roundabout way of doing it, however, because, as she herself explains, she wanted to leave herself a way of retreat. There was another reason for her choosing this indirect way of intimating to Chekhov her readiness to divorce her husband : her all too justified doubt whether Chekhov would accept her sacrifice. He could certainly not afford to keep his family as well as her and her three children, even if her husband had agreed to let her have them. Be that as it may, the fact remains that it was her roundabout way of telling Chekhov of her intention to leave her husband that Chekhov made use of in *The Seagull*. Lydia bought a pendant for a watch-chain and had it engraved on one side : " Short Stories by A. Chekhov," and on the other, " Page 267, lines 6 and 7 ". The lines, taken from Chekhov's story *The Neighbours*, and since made famous in *The Seagull*, read, " If you ever want my life, come and take it." But Chekhov remained unresponsive. He would not even acknowledge the receipt of the pendant. Instead, he included the incident in *The Seagull*, a play that is remarkable for its many themes which Chekhov must have taken from all sorts of sources, but which, in the light of Lydia Avilova's memoirs, is also of great biographical value. Chekhov had met Lydia at a mask ball where he told her that his play contained a message for her. Lydia fastened on the episode with the medallion as containing that message, as well she might, considering that it was she who was mainly responsible for it. She soon tumbled to the fact that the different numbers Chekhov had used for the pages and lines of Nina's message to Trigorin referred to her own book of short stories, but the sentence in her book, " It is improper for young ladies to go to mask balls," while no doubt entirely in keeping with Chekhov's habit of countering a serious situation with a joke and while it did convey the information that he had known all along that he was speaking to her at the mask ball, was, surely, not the reply " to many things " he had promised to give her in *The Seagull*. Chekhov's real message to her seems to be contained in the unhappy ending of Nina's love affair, the obvious conclusion being that if a young girl's love could come to grief, then how could she, a mother of three children, expect a happier ending to their love. It was Chekhov's typical way of justifying himself for refusing to accept Lydia's sacrifice, for his insight into the heart of man must have told him that a happy conclusion to their love affair was scarcely likely. " He knew everything; he understood everything," Lydia herself repeatedly writes.

The autobiographical elements in *The Seagull* were, till the publication of Lydia Avilova's memoirs, generally taken by Russian critics to refer to Lydia Mizinov, a beautiful young girl with ash-blonde hair who was a friend of Chekhov's sister Mary and a frequent visitor to Melikhovo, where she also met Chekhov's writer friend Potapenko. Nemirovich-Danchenko, one of the founders of the Moscow Art Theatre who was mainly instrumental in putting on *The Seagull* at what was at the beginning known as The People's Art Theatre, was the first to draw this conclusion, though with certain reservations. " Many people had thought," he writes in his reminiscences of Chekhov, " that Trigorin in *The Seagull* was autobiographical. Tolstoy had said something to that effect, too. But it always seemed to me that it was Potapenko who served as the model for Trigorin. Nina Zarechnaya gives Trigorin a medallion on which is engraved a sentence from one of Trigorin's stories : ' If you ever want my life, come and take it.' " (As we have seen, Nemirovich-Danchenko is not only wrong about the fact that the *sentence* had been engraved on the medallion—a curious mistake to make—but he also had no idea of the circumstances which led Chekhov to use the medallion episode.) " This sentence," he goes on, " is actually taken from one of Chekhov's stories, and it expresses very well the simplicity and self-sacrifice which is so characteristic of Chekhov's heroines. This gave people the excuse for associating Trigorin with Chekhov. But Chekhov may have grown fond of this strong and at the same time tender expression of a woman's loyalty and wished to repeat it. For a proper understanding of Trigorin's character it is more important to take into account his attitude to women, which in no way resembles Chekhov's own attitude, but is much more like Potapenko's. In general, of course, it is neither the one nor the other, but anyone you like.

" *The Seagull*," Nemirovich-Danchenko goes on, " is an extraordinarily sincere piece of work, and many of its details may have been taken straight from Chekhov's life in Melikhovo. Even the name of the girl, a friend of Chekhov's sister, who served Chekhov as the model for Nina Zarechnaya, has been mentioned. But here, too, the similarity is purely accidental. There were hundreds of such girls in Russia at the time, and all of them were anxious to leave their homes in some dull place in the provinces to find some work to which they could devote themselves ' wholly ', and to sacrifice themselves entirely to ' him '—the man of talent who had roused their imagination. There were lots of such girls in our country when women were deprived of their rights."

A modern Russian critic, V. Yermilov,* goes much further than Nemirovich-Danchenko in associating Lydia (Leeka) Mizinov with Nina Zarechnaya. He points out that Leeka was an exceptionally good-looking girl who was in love with

* Драматургия Чехова. (Chekhov's Drama), Moscow, 1948.

Chekhov and, in spite of all the facts that point to the contrary, asserts that Chekhov was also in love with her. He quotes Leeka's letter to Chekhov in which she more than hints at her love for him. " You know perfectly well," Leeka wrote, " how I feel about you, and I am not in the least ashamed to write about it. I also know that your attitude towards me is one of condescension and indifference. My dearest wish is to cure myself of the terrible condition in which I am now, but it is very difficult for me to do it by myself. I implore you to help me. Please do not ask me to come to see you and do not try to see me. This means nothing to you, but it may help me to forget you. . . ." There is no hint in this letter of any reciprocity of feeling on the part of Chekhov, but that does not deter Yermilov from insisting that Chekhov did reciprocate her feeling but did nothing about it because he was afraid that a " great " love would interfere with his writings! However, Leeka soon got over her infatuation for Chekhov and turned for solace to Potapenko who did not scruple to sacrifice a young girl's devotion for the sake of his own gratification. Curiously enough, Leeka's fate did in the end resemble Nina Zarechnaya's—she had a child by Potapenko who eventually left her—but that did not happen till three years *after* the publication of *The Seagull*.

Yermilov's theory that " the story of Leeka's unhappy love explains the genesis of *The Seagull* and the secret of the origin of the chief characters of the play " and that Trigorin, furthermore, was a sort of amalgam of Chekhov and Potapenko, can hardly be defended in view of what we now know from Lydia Avilova's memoirs. To search for autobiographical details in the character of Trigorin is a thankless task. Some of Trigorin's speeches certainly have an autobiographical ring. For instance, his long speech to Nina in the second act in which he tells her at great length of a writer's incessant worries about the plots of his stories. That may be an echo from Chekhov's early days as a writer when he was writing a different story almost every second day. But so are Konstantin's speeches about the need of new forms in art which to a certain extent at least, particularly in their application to the theatre, are the expression of Chekhov's own views. But as regards the *character* of Trigorin, Chekhov no doubt created it as any other great writer creates his characters, by drawing on his own experience of life and transmuting it into art. Nemirovich-Danchenko was quite right: there may be a bit of Chekhov, and a bit of Potapenko, and a bit of someone else in Trigorin, but it would be a mistake to identify him with Chekhov or Potapenko or indeed with the two of them. For in the final analysis Trigorin is a highly individualised character who is just himself. The same is true of Nina, who is neither Lydia Mizinov nor Lydia Avilova, but a completely realised individual portrait of a girl who is strong-minded enough to stick to her chosen career as an actress in spite of the disasters in her private life.

Chekhov's name was associated with another woman, who is mentioned in Lydia Avilova's memoirs. It was the actress Lydia Yavorskaya (the name of Lydia certainly seems to have had some strange significance in its association with Chekhov). But all the gossip about her and Chekhov was as little justified as the stories about Lydia Mizinov. Yavorskaya was a friend of Shchepkina-Kupernik, a writer and translator of Shakespeare, who was a great friend of Chekhov's sister and of Chekhov himself. It was Shchepkina-Kupernik who introduced her to Chekhov, and there is a photograph of Chekhov, Yavorskaya and Shchepkina-Kupernik in existence. Chekhov is also known to have read *The Seagull* to Yavorskaya in

Melikhovo. Describing Chekhov's relations with Yavorskaya, Shchepkina-Kupernik writes : " There was something odd about Chekhov's relations with Yavorskaya : one day he seemed to like her and another day he didn't, but she certainly interested him as a woman. He was the first to recommend her as an actress to Suvorin, whose theatre she subsequently joined, and he went to see the plays in which she acted. Their relations were certainly not as simple as his and mine. There was a sort of flirtation going on. I remember she once played the heroine in an Indian drama in which—with blue lotus flowers behind her ears—she knelt before her chosen one and said to him, ' My only one, my inscrutable one, my wonderful one. . . .' And whenever Chekhov entered her blue drawing-room, she would assume the pose of the Indian heroine and, with hands outstretched towards him, declaim, ' My only one, my great one, my wonderful one. . . .' An echo of this I later found in *The Seagull* where Arkadina kneels before Trigorin and calls him her only one, her great one, and so on. Her parts, too, found their way into *The Seagull*, such as *La dame aux camélias* and *Life's Whirl.* . . . But there was nothing more than a superficial similarity there."

Yavorskaya's theatrical pose when Chekhov entered her drawing-room hardly shows any serious attachment between the two, but the Moscow gossips were busy, and it is interesting that Chekhov denied the whole affair to another friend, the writer Lazarev-Gruzinsky. " At the time of her acquaintance with Chekhov," Lazarev-Gruzinsky writes, " Yavorskaya was playing in the Moscow theatre of Korsh. She was a beautiful and a very charming woman, not a brilliant but a very fascinating comedy actress. Thanks to her talented acting, Sardou's play *Madame Sans-Gêne* ran for over a hundred performances in one season at Korsh's theatre. . . . One day on entering the theatre for free tickets for the newspaper I worked on at the time, I saw Chekhov emerging from somewhere behind the scenes.

" ' Good heavens,' I said to him in surprise, ' what are you doing here ? I thought you were in Melikhovo. Oh, I see! I forgot you were paying court to Yavorskaya! '

" ' Oh? Who told you that ? '

" ' Why, the whole of Moscow is talking about it! '

" ' *Tout Moscou, tout Moscou!* ' Chekhov laughed, and he went on to deny the rumour emphatically."

But the scandalmongers were not so easily silenced and very soon the story went round that Chekhov, jilted by Yavorskaya, had written a skit on her in his short story *Ariadne*. But, as Lazarev-Gruzinsky rightly surmises, that rumour may well have been started by Yavorskaya herself who, he observes, " was first of all an actress, and, being an actress, loved publicity."

The rumours, however, reached Petersburg, and Lydia Avilova heard of it, too, as she was not slow in reminding Chekhov at the mask ball.

Lydia Avilova's description of the first night of *The Seagull* at the Alexandrinsky Theatre in Petersburg on 29th October 1896 is by far the best account of that scandalous occurrence in the history of the Russian theatre. Many things contributed to the play's failure and Chekhov's flight from Petersburg, not the least of which was that the play had been put on for the benefit night of the light comedy actress Levkeyeva, who did not appear in it herself but whose public was hardly of the right sort to appreciate a play by Chekhov, and particularly so poetic a play as *The Seagull*. Lydia Avilova, however, is probably right in ascribing a large part of the play's failure to the professional jealousy of the Petersburg literary set, to whom Chekhov's rise to fame at an age when most of them had still to struggle hard for recognition was a constant cause of small-minded pique and ill-will.

In March 1897 Chekhov's first serious haemorrhage occurred. In that year *Uncle Vanya* was published, but Chekhov was still unknown as a playwright, *The Seagull* had still to be produced by the Moscow Art Theatre, and his two last plays, *The Three Sisters* and *The Cherry Orchard*, had still to be written. Chekhov had hurried to Moscow to meet Lydia Avilova although he had been feeling ill. The rest is described very movingly by Lydia Avilova in her memoirs, to which little need be added, except perhaps to fill in the background of the incident with the flowers Lydia had brought Chekhov and Tolstoy's rather unfortunate visit to the private clinic on 28th March.

The incident with the flowers is characteristic as showing how careful Chekhov was to protect Lydia's reputation. In his letter to Lydia from the clinic Chekhov wrote: " Your flowers do not fade but are getting lovelier." But when the writer Shcheglov went to see Chekhov at the clinic and ventured a guess that the flowers at Chekhov's bedside had probably been sent by some Moscow lady admirer of his, Chekhov immediately replied, " You are wrong. They're not from a female but from a male admirer of mine, a Moscow millionaire," and (Shcheglov writes) he added with a bitter smile, " He sends me flowers, but were I to ask him for a loan of ten roubles, he wouldn't give it to me. As if I didn't know them—those male admirers!" Actually, Chekhov had only once in his life asked a millionaire for a loan and, having got it, he could not rest until he had repaid it.

Tolstoy, afflicted by the blindness that is so characteristic of men who believe they have discovered a simple panacea for all human ills, did not hesitate, when he called on Chekhov at the clinic, to make use of the opportunity to enrol Chekhov among his disciples. His visit, however, had the disastrous effect that usually attended Tolstoy's efforts to save those dear to him : Chekhov suffered a bad relapse. It is significant of Chekhov's relations with Lydia Avilova that it should have been she who had asked Tolstoy to go and see him. Again and again it was either Lydia or Chekhov who from the best imaginable motives inflicted pain on one another.

Chekhov did not share Tolstoy's religious views, but he was very fond of " the crafty old man ", as he called the author of *War and Peace*. During Tolstoy's serious illness in 1900, Chekhov told a friend : " I fear Tolstoy's death, for it would leave an empty place in my life. For one thing, I like him more than any other man, and for another, while there is still a Tolstoy in literature, it is pleasant to be a literary man even if you know very well that you have not accomplished anything and are not likely to accomplish anything. Such a thought is not so terrifying because Tolstoy does enough for everybody. Then again, Tolstoy's position is impregnable, the authority he enjoys is enormous, and while he is alive bad taste in literature and every sort of vulgarity, spite, and self-conceit will never dare to show themselves in the open. Only his moral authority can keep the so-called literary moods and movements at a certain high level. . . ."

Chekhov always took Tolstoy's strictures on his work as a playwright in good part. In 1902 in Yalta he suddenly interrupted a literary discussion among some writers who had come to visit him by declaring gloomily (like a born humorist, Chekhov always looked gloomy when about to crack a joke), " This year I shan't publish any new play ! " And when asked to explain this startling announcement, he said, " Tolstoy has made me change my mind about writing any more plays. I asked him once whether he liked my plays. 'No,' he replied, 'I don't like them!' 'Why not?' 'Because they're even worse than Shakespeare's!'"

Tolstoy said the same thing to Lydia, but unfortunately he went to visit Chekhov at the clinic. This is how Shcheglov describes Chekhov's account of Tolstoy's visit:

"'Do you know who came to see me yesterday?' Chekhov said suddenly, looking very pleased.

"'No, I'm afraid I don't.'

"'Leo Tolstoy!'

"I could not help feeling excited. 'What did you talk about?' I asked.

"Chekhov frowned a little and replied evasively:

"'I didn't talk a lot to him as I'm not allowed to talk much, and, besides, however much I respect Tolstoy, I don't agree with him about—many things!' he underlined with unconcealed agitation which brought on a fit of coughing.

"It was clear," Shcheglov adds, "that Chekhov was pleased and touched that Tolstoy had been to see him but not by the moral effect of Tolstoy's visit, and it was no less clear that . . . Tolstoy's preaching at the bedside of a sick and impecunious writer had been most inopportune."

Chekhov himself described the effect of Tolstoy's visit on him in a letter to Suvorin. "The author of *Ward 6*," he wrote, "was transferred from Ward 16 to Ward 14. It is spacious here. Two windows, three tables. Not much blood. The morning after Tolstoy came to see me (we had a long talk together), at four o'clock, I had another serious haemorrhage."

On her return to Petersburg Lydia Avilova had a dream in the train, and this terrible dream perhaps explains more than anything else the tragedy of their relationship. A year later she had a letter from Chekhov in which he, in his usual veiled manner, drew her attention to his last story *About Love*. This time Chekhov went so far as to give the heroine of his story the same patronymic as Lydia's : Anna *Alexeyevna*. But his appeal to the " higher motives " which should determine the conduct of a man who is in love with a married woman with children, as might have been expected, merely made Lydia angry (she was also vexed that Chekhov should have written such a *short* story about her) and she wrote him a furious letter, which made Chekhov seek refuge in his usual veiled jocularity.

On her next visit to Moscow Chekhov, who had already sold his small estate, was living in Yalta. He wanted to buy a house in Moscow for his mother and sister (his father had died shortly before that on 12th October 1898), and he asked Lydia to find a suitable house for him. Nothing came of it, however, because in the end Chekhov could not afford to buy the house. Their last meeting took place on the Moscow railway station in May 1899, ten years after their first meeting, on the day of the special performance of *The Seagull* which the Moscow Art Theatre had arranged for him. The meeting is described in detail by Lydia Avilova. The significant thing about it is, surely, that Chekhov should have been so anxious that she should accompany him to the performance of *The Seagull*. Was he so anxious about it because he wanted that she who had witnessed the terrible failure of the play, should now see it performed by a company that had made such a great success of it ? Or was there some other motive, something that went deeper and concerned both of them more intimately ? Whatever the reason, it was not to be, and for the second time—once at the clinic when she had refused to stay one more day in Moscow and now at the railway station—

Lydia refused a request from Chekhov that seemed particularly important to him. The reasons she gave for her refusal were trifling on both occasions, but also so perfectly in keeping with what Chekhov took as his motto as a writer—"life as it is." And nothing Chekhov himself has written is so full of that heartbreaking melancholy as that last meeting with the woman who had exercised so strong an influence on his feelings through most of his active life. The sweets he had brought for her children, his dandling of little Nina, his anger with Lydia for reminding him that he was an invalid, his fear that she might catch a cold in her spring costume, and, finally, the way he walked off without looking round as the train began to move out of the station. It was all over.

That day he saw a performance of *The Seagull* and realised to his horror that it was not the play he had written. That was something he had experienced before and was to experience later. On that occasion he was so appalled that he poured out his heart to Olga Knipper, the young actress who played the part of Arkardina and whom he was to marry two years later. Three years after his marriage, on 15th July, 1904, at the Black Forest spa of Badenweiler, he died.

" He woke up in the early hours of the morning," his wife writes, " and for the first time asked me to send for the doctor. When the doctor came, he ordered some champagne for him. Chekhov sat up and said to the doctor in German in a loud and rather significant voice, ' *Ich sterbe*'. Then he took the glass, turned his face to me, and with his wonderful smile said, ' It is a long time since I drank champagne. . . .' He then quietly drank his champagne, lay down on his left side, and soon grew silent for ever. . . ."

D. M.

CHEKHOV IN MY LIFE

ONE

ON THE 24th of January 1889 I received a note from my sister : " Come at once. Chekhov is here." My sister was married to the editor and publisher of a daily newspaper with a very large circulation. She was much older than I. Small, fair, with large dreamy eyes and tiny hands and feet, she always aroused in me feelings of envy and tenderness. Beside her I seemed to be too rosy-cheeked, tall, and plump. . . . Besides, I was born and bred in Moscow and had only lived in Petersburg for just over a year. My sister's house was always full of celebrities : actors, painters, singers, poets, writers. And her whole past, her romantic marriage with an " elopement " straight from a dance, while our father, who disliked her lover, would not let her out of his sight, invested her in my eyes with a kind of magic halo. I had only just married a young university graduate who occupied the position of an assistant secretary at the Ministry of Education. What was there in my past? Just unrealised dreams. . . .

One of my dreams was to become a writer. I had been writing both verse and prose ever since I was a child. I cared for nothing so much in my life as for writing. Literature was everything in the world to me; I read a lot, and among my favourite authors Chekhonte* did not by any means occupy the last place. His stories, incidentally, appeared also in the paper edited by my brother-in-law, and every story of his aroused my enthusiasm. How I cried over Jonah in Chekhov's story *Anguish*, the old cabby who confided his sorrow to his ancient mare because there was no one in the world who cared to listen to him. He had only had one son and—he was dead. And no one cared. But why was it that now that Chekhov had written the story everyone began to care, and everyone read it and many cried over it? Oh, the all-powerful magic of the artist's word!

" Come at once. Chekhov is here! " I was at the time nursing my baby son Lyovushka who was already nine months old, and I was free the whole evening because after his bath he slept quietly for a long time, and, besides, I had an old nurse I could rely on. She had been my nanny too.

Michael (my husband) was busy, and he was not particularly interested in meeting Chekhov. So I went alone.

He was walking up and down my brother-in-law's study and seemed to be telling some story, but, on seeing me in the door-way, he stopped.

" Ah, Miss Flora," said Sergey, my brother-in-law, in a loud voice. " Let me introduce you to Miss Flora. A protégée of mine."

* Chekhov's pseudonym during the first years of his literary career. (D.M.)

Chekhov came up to me quickly and held my hand in his with a tender smile. We looked at each other, and I couldn't help feeling that he was surprised at something. I supposed it must have been at the name of Flora. Sergey called me that because of my fresh complexion and luxuriant hair which at the time I used to wear in two long thick plaits.

" She knows your stories by heart," Sergey went on, " and I daresay she must have written you hundreds of letters. But she keeps it a secret. Too shy to confess."

I noticed that Chekhov's eyes seemed to be slightly screwed up. His stiff white collar hung like a horse-collar about his neck, and his tie was far from beautiful.

When I sat down, he began walking up and down the room again and went on with his story. I gathered that he had come to Petersburg to put on his play *Ivanov*, but that he was very dissatisfied with the actors, that he failed to recognise his characters in them, and that he felt that his play would be a failure. He confessed that he was so worried and so much in despair about it that he was coughing up blood. And, besides, he disliked Petersburg. He wished he could finish his business and go back. He vowed never again to write for the stage. Not that he had anything to say against the actors. They were excellent, and they played excellently, but what they played had nothing to do with his characters but was something of their own.

My sister Nadya came in to tell us that dinner was served. Sergey got up, and his visitors followed suit. We went to the dining-room where two tables had been laid, one—the large one—for dinner, and the other had bottles and snacks on it. I remained standing at the wall away from the rest. Chekhov came up to me with a plate in his hand and took hold of one of my plaits.

31

" I've never seen plaits like these before," he said.

I thought he behaved so familiarly with me because I was just some Miss Flora, a protégée of my brother-in-law's. If he had known Michael and that I had almost a year-old son, he'd . . .

At the table Chekhov sat next to me.

" She also writes," Sergey informed Chekhov with a condescending air. " She has something—a spark—and—er—ideas. . . . Not much, but still there is some idea in each of her stories."

Chekhov turned to me and smiled.

" A writer ought to write about what he sees and feels," he said. " Sincerely. Truthfully. I'm often asked what I meant to express by a story. I never reply to such questions. My business is to write. And," he added with a smile, " I can write about anything you like. Ask me to write a story about this bottle and I will write you a story under the title of *A Bottle*. Living images create thought, but thought does not create images."

And after listening to some flattering objection from one of the guests, he frowned a little and leant against the back of the chair.

" Quite right," he said. " A writer is not a little twittering bird, but who said that I wanted him to twitter ? If I live, think, fight, and suffer, then all this is reflected in whatever I happen to write. . . . I will describe life to you truthfully, that is, artistically, and you will see in it what you have not seen before, what you never noticed before : its divergence from the norm, its contradictions. . . ." He unexpectedly turned to me with a question. " Will you be at the first night of *Ivanov* ? " he asked.

" I don't think so. I don't expect it will be so easy to get a ticket."

" I'll send you one," he said quickly. " Do you live here ?
With Mr. Khudekov ? "

I laughed.

" At last I can tell you that I'm not Miss Flora or a protégée
of Mr. Khudekov's. He calls me that for fun. I'm Mrs. Khudekov's sister and—just imagine it!—I'm married and the mother
of a family. And as I'm feeding my child, I'm afraid I shall
have to hurry home now."

Sergey heard what I said and shouted to me :

" Miss Flora, they'll send for you if you're wanted. She lives
only a few minutes from here," he explained to Chekhov.
" Sit down. Your little brat is asleep. Don't let her go, Mr.
Chekhov."

Chekhov bent down and looked into my eyes.

" You have a son ? " he said. " How nice! "

How difficult it is sometimes to explain and even to perceive
the true meaning of some happening. And as a matter of fact
nothing did actually happen. We simply looked closely into
each other's eyes. But how much there was in the look we had
exchanged! I felt as if something had burst in my soul, as if
some rocket had exploded there brightly, joyfully, trium-
phantly, rapturously. I had no doubt that Chekhov felt the
same, and we looked at each other surprised and happy.

" I'll be coming here again," said Chekhov. " We shall
meet, shan't we ? Let me have everything you've written or
published. I promise to read it all very carefully. All right ? "

When I came home, I found nanny swaddling Lyovushka,
who was frowning and grunting, as though about to burst out
crying any moment.

" Have I a son ? How nice! " I said to him, laughing and
feeling very happy.

Michael followed me into the nursery.

" Have a good look at yourself in the glass," he said crossly. " Red and dishevelled. And what a silly way to wear your plaits. Wanted to impress your Chekhov, I suppose. Lyovushka is crying and his mother is flirting with some literary gentleman."

To Michael a " literary gentleman " was synonymous with a windbag. I knew that.

" Is Chekhov a literary gentleman ? " I asked drily.

And I felt as though everything inside me went dead. I felt as though the great happiness that lit up my world so brightly were quietly folding its wings. . . . It was all over. Everything was just as before. Why should life be simple and beautiful? Who said it should ?

TWO

THREE years passed after my first meeting with Chekhov. I often remembered him and always with a gentle feeling of dreamy sadness. I already had three children : Lyova, Lodya, and a baby girl Nina. Michael was an exemplary husband. To add to his earnings, he obtained some work for the evenings and spent all his free time nursing and playing with the children.

There could be no doubt that our family happiness had grown stronger. One day Michael said to me, " Well, mother, so they've clipped your wings, have they ? " I had wanted to devote myself to literature. Goltsev* once asked me to bring him everything I had written, and later he made me apply myself seriously to writing. He explained to me what was wrong with my stories and demanded that I should rewrite

* Editor of the Moscow monthly *Russian Thought* to which Chekhov contributed many of his stories. (D.M.)

them. Sometimes he would say to me, " This is very good. Good enough to be published. But it's a little too soon for you. Work a little more." When I told him that I was going to be married, he was dismayed and said, " Well, it's all over now. You won't ever be a writer now." It was then that I vowed to go on working and promised myself that my marriage would never interfere with my writing. But I was mistaken. My married life did not seem to leave me any time for literary work. Michael was at the Ministry every day and came home only at dinner-time. It would seem that I had nothing to do all day and that I could spend my free time as I liked, all the more so as I had a maid and a cook. But it only seemed so. The whole day was spent in trifles : I had to do my shopping and buy our food where Michael told me : coffee on Morskaya Street, cream on Sadovaya Street, tobacco on Nevsky Avenue, *kvas* on Mokhovaya Street, and so on. And I had to prepare the sauce for the roast myself and not leave it to the cook. I had also to make his cigarettes. But the chief worry of my life was the doors. I had to see that the doors were properly closed all day so that there was no smell of cooking in the living-rooms ; and in the evening they had to be opened wide so as to make quite sure that our flat was properly aired. And woe to me if, on coming home from the office, Michael caught the slightest whiff from the kitchen. When Michael sat down to write his thesis one evening, I went to the bedroom and sat down at my manuscript, but almost immediately there was a shout, " Why is the bedroom door closed ? Open it ! And what are you doing there ? Come here ! "

" I want to write."

" You want to, but I have to. I've got all muddled up in a sentence here. Come, help me to put it right, literary lady."

Or he would start pacing the room and whistling some tune.

When I proposed that we should separate, he said :

" Why should we ? Just think, old girl. All our misunderstandings and quarrels are only caused by your obstinacy. You are used to living an irregular sort of life. Doing just what you like, what your sweet fancy tells you. You think this is freedom, but in my opinion it's a disorderly way of living. My work at the office bores me stiff, but I have to carry on with it because you want to live in town and not in the country where I could have been living the life of a country gentleman. I got reconciled to your idea of living in town, so why can't you get reconciled to the idea of keeping house for me and seeing that everything is done properly ? Do you really want me to go on telling you how beautiful you are ? Paying you all sorts of compliments ? And it's you who want a divorce ! Why ? You ought to be ashamed of yourself. . . ! "

I knew perfectly well that he loved me more and not less than before, and that he could not live without me. And, besides, we were already expecting our first baby, and both of us wanted a child badly.

And the birth of our little boy brought us " family happiness ". We were no longer fighting each other as before. We were more ready to compromise. Then two more children were born to us, and there could no longer be any talk of separation or divorce. My " wings " were " clipped ", and Michael had to work very hard to provide for the family.

During these three years we got used to each other, we became friends, and I found it easier to put up with Michael's angry outbursts, particularly as he was always very sorry afterwards and did his best to make amends. He almost stopped interfering with my writing in my free time, and my stories began to appear in print. So my life now seemed to be very full and often, when the children were not ill, happy.

I could not help feeling terribly bored, though.

THREE

In January 1892 Sergey was celebrating the twenty-fifth anniversary of the foundation of his newspaper. The celebrations were to begin with a religious service, and then the guests were to be invited to the drawing-room where a long table was laid for dinner. There was no room for all the guests in the dining-room, and that was why everything there had been prepared for the service.

To get from the drawing-room to the dining-room one had to cross a landing at the top of the stairs leading from the entrance hall. The wall opposite the stairs was covered by a huge looking-glass. I stood at the door of the drawing-room and, without being seen myself, I could see in the glass all the people who were coming up the stairs before they reached the landing. There were men and women among them, some of whom I did and some I did not know, and I could not help feeling depressed as I thought of the boring day ahead of me.

I should probably be placed at the table next to some important person whom I would have to entertain, and the dinner was sure to go on for hours and all the time I should have to rack my brains for some interesting topic of conversation and do my best to appear pleasant and vivacious.

Suddenly I saw in the glass two men ascending the stairs. It sometimes happens that one look is enough to fix a scene in one's mind so that it remains there for the rest of one's life. I can see now Suvorin's unattractive head and next to it the young and sweet face of Chekhov. He raised his right hand and brushed back a strand of hair. His eyes were slightly screwed up, and his lips were moving almost imperceptibly. He must have been saying something, but I could not hear anything. They were just in time for the beginning of the religious service. Everybody crowded into the dining-room, the singing began, and I, too, joined the crowd. And while the service and the singing went on, I called to mind my first meeting with Chekhov and that inexplicable and strangely unreal feeling which suddenly made us so close to one another. I was wondering whether he would recognise me now. Would he remember ? Would that intimate feeling of closeness be re-born again in us, the feeling which three years ago blazed up so brightly in my soul ?

We ran into each other accidentally in the crowd and at once stretched out our hands to one another happily.

" I did not expect to see you here," I said.

" But I did," he replied. " And do you know what ? Let's sit down together as we did before. All right ? "

We went into the drawing-room together.

" Shall we choose a place ? "

" I'm afraid it's no good," I said. " You will be put in accordance with your eminent position among the galaxy of talents. I mean, as near to my brother-in-law as possible."

" But think how nice it would be if we could sit here, in this corner by the window. Don't you agree ? "

" Oh, I do, but they won't let us. They'll drag you away."

" But I shan't let them," Chekhov said, laughing. " I shan't give in."

We sat down, laughing and encouraging each other to resist any attempt to separate us.

" And where's Mr. Chekhov ? " Sergey asked suddenly in a loud voice. " Anton Pavlovich, may I ask you——"

My sister Nadya was also looking for Chekhov and calling him by name.

Chekhov raised himself a little in his chair and silently brushed back his hair.

" Ah, so that's where you are! But there's also a place for your lady next to you here. Please . . ."

" Oh, leave them alone," Nadya said unexpectedly. " If they like it better there . . ."

Sergey laughed, and they left us alone.

" You see how beautifully everything's turned out ? " said Chekhov. " We've won."

" Do you know lots of people here ? " I asked.

" But didn't it seem to you," Chekhov said, without answering my question, " didn't it seem to you that when we met three years ago we didn't just get acquainted with each other, but found each other after a long separation ? "

" Well, yes. . . ." I replied doubtfully.

" Of course! I know. Such a feeling can only be reciprocal. I experienced it for the first time and I could not forget it. A feeling that we've known each other intimately a long time.

And, you know, I feel it's so strange that in spite of it I should know so little about you and you about me."

" Why so strange ? Ours was a very, very long separation. Don't forget it wasn't in this life, but in a life long forgotten."

" And what were we to each other in that life ? " asked Chekhov.

" Not husband and wife, I'm sure," I hastily replied.

We both laughed.

" But we were in love with each other. Don't you think so ? We were very young and—we perished in a—shipwreck! " Chekhov let his imagination run away with him.

" Oh, I do seem to remember something! " I said, laughing.

" Ah, there you are. You see, I'm right. We had a long struggle with the waves. Your arm was round my neck. . . ."

" That was because I was in such an awful panic. You see, I can't swim. So it seems that I drowned you."

" Well, to tell you the truth I'm not a good swimmer, either. Very likely it was I who went under first and dragged you after me."

" I don't blame you for that. The important thing is that we've now met as friends."

" And you still trust me utterly ? "

" But how can I trust you ? " I said in surprise. " You drowned me instead of saving me."

" But why didn't you let go of my neck ? "

The people at the table did not forget Chekhov. They often shouted remarks to him or asked him questions, exchanged greetings with him or paid him compliments.

" I was just saying to my neighbour what a delightful thing your story is. . . . A real *bonbon*! "

42

This *bonbon* made us laugh, and we could not look at each other for a long time without laughing.

" And how I waited for you," I suddenly remembered. " How I waited for you! I mean, when I still lived in Moscow. Before my marriage."

" Why did you wait for me ? " Chekhov seemed surprised.

" Because I wanted to know you so badly and a friend of my brother's, a man called Popov, told me that he often saw you and that you were such a nice man and wouldn't refuse him if he asked you to come and see us. But you did not come."

" Tell that Popov of yours, whom I don't remember having ever met, that he's my worst enemy," Chekhov said seriously.

And we started talking about Moscow, Goltsev, and *Russian Thought*.

" I don't like Petersburg," Chekhov repeated. " It's so cold and so damp. And you, too, aren't kind. Why didn't you send me anything ? I asked you specially. Remember ? I asked you to send me your stories."

People started coming up to clink glasses. . . . Chekhov got up, brushed back his hair, and listened with lowered eyes to the compliments and good wishes. He then sat down with a sigh of relief.

" That's fame for you," I said.

" To hell with it," said Chekhov. " I'm sure most of them never read a line of what I've written. And if they did read me, they most probably abused me. What I want now is not words but music. Why isn't there any music ? We should have had a Roumanian band. Must have music. And how old are you ? " he asked me suddenly.

" Twenty-eight."

" And I'm thirty-two. When we first met we were three years younger : twenty-five and twenty-nine. How young we were ! "

43

" I wasn't twenty-five then, and I'm not really twenty-eight.
I shall be in May, though."

" And I'm thirty-two. What a pity."

" My husband often reminds me that I'm no longer a young
girl. He always adds two years to my age. That's why I too
add on a little."

" Not young ? At twenty-seven ? "

People began rising from the table. The dinner lasted three
hours, but it passed quickly for me. I saw Michael who was
trying to get through the crowd to me and I noticed at once
that he was in a bad mood.

" I'm going home," Michael said. " And you ? "

I told him that I intended to stay.

" Of course," he said.

But I felt that I ought to introduce him to Chekhov.

They shook hands. I was not surprised to see the cold,
almost hostile, look on Michael's face, but I was surprised at
Chekhov : at first he tried to smile, but his smile did not come
off, and he tossed back his head with a proud movement. They
did not say a word to each other, and Michael went away at
once.

I stayed behind, but not for long : the guests were in a hurry
to leave.

At home a storm was brewing. Michael did not like our
vivacious talk at dinner and he was angry that we should have
refused to take the places reserved for us.

But at the time I did not know what was awaiting me.

An obliging friend told Michael that after the anniversary
dinner Chekhov went to a restaurant with some friends where
he got drunk and boasted he'd take me away from my husband,
make me get a divorce, and marry me. His friends were said
to have encouraged him, promised to help him, and almost

carried him on their shoulders in their enthusiasm. Michael was furious with indignation.

I felt utterly stunned. But when I recovered a little and was able to think clearly, I said to myself, It can't be true! Someone must have invented the story out of malice in order to blacken Chekhov's character in my eyes and incite Michael against him. But who would have wished to do such a thing ? I decided that Michael could have heard the story from one of two persons. One was above suspicion, as for the other . . . And I at once remembered that the other person was sitting opposite us at the dinner-table, a few places away, and that he looked sullen. He was the author of a number of long novels, but no one took any notice of him and he was not asked to sit at the top of the table. He addressed Chekhov in very flattering language, expressed his admiration for his works, but there was no doubt that he envied him to the point of hatred, and I found out later that that was true.

After dinner he had said to me in passing, " I've never seen you so animated."

" It's him," I decided. " Of course, it's him. I'm certain. He invented it all. Made it all up and spread it all over the town." I made enquiries and found out that he was present at the restaurant on the night of the anniversary dinner. I told Michael about my theory.

" Made it all up ? Possibly. Yes, it was he who told me," Michael confessed. " But everyone knows what a swine he is."

I felt awfully relieved.

When I said good-bye to Chekhov I promised to write and send him my stories, and now I decided that it could be done, but I could not help reproaching him for his indiscretion. He replied immediately :

" Your letter both distressed and perplexed me. What does it all mean ? My dignity does not permit me to justify myself and, besides, your accusation is so vague that I don't know what exactly I ought to apologise for. But from what I gather it has something to do with a story someone spread about me. Am I right ?

" I ask you earnestly (if you trust me as much as the people who are spreading those stories about me) not to believe anything people in your Petersburg tell you. Or, if you can't help believing them, then believe everything they say about me : that I'm married to an heiress, that the wives of my best friends are my mistresses, etc. For goodness' sake, calm yourself! However, what does it matter ? To defend myself against gossip is . . . useless. Think what you like of me. . . .

" . . . I'm living in the country. It's cold. I'm shovelling snow into the pond and I'm thinking with pleasure of my decision never to come to Petersburg again."

This was the beginning of my correspondence with Chekhov. I was terribly upset at his decision not to come to Petersburg. Did it mean that I would never see him again ? Would there be no more bright days in my " happy family life ? "

And every time my heart contracted painfully at that thought.

FOUR

DURING those rare intervals when everything was all right at home—the children well, Michael calm and in a good humour—the thought often occurred to me that at the time I was probably experiencing the greatest happiness that fate had in store for me. It is true there were also my literary successes that made me feel happy—and Chekhov's letters. But I did not have time to write a lot or too often because my children were ill, either all of them together or singly, and when that happened I could think only of them and devote all my time, both by day and by night, only to them. Besides, Michael's unfortunate character would get the better of him against his will so suddenly that it was quite impossible for me to do anything about it or to avoid a scene. And that always made me terribly unhappy.

Chekhov's letters I received in secret, at the post office, poste restante, and I did it because I was afraid that a letter would arrive while I was out and at an inopportune moment. But Michael knew of our correspondence, and I sometimes gave him some of Chekhov's letters to read.

" You can see how useful they are. His advice is a great help to me. . . ."

" I can imagine the rubbish you write to him. That's what I'd like to read. Will you let me see your letters ? Will you ? "

No. I did not let him see my letters.

One day my sister came to see me.

" Try and come to us tonight without Michael," she said with a sly smile. " But remember! Without Michael."

" Why ? " I could not help asking her in surprise.

" You'll see. You know what I'm thinking about ? I bet you'll never guess. A boring story."

" I don't know what you're talking about."

" Well, *A Boring Story*. Haven't you read it ? "

" Of course. But what are you driving at ? "

" You remember there was a bottle of champagne there, cheese. . . ."

" Are you expecting Chekhov . . . tonight ? "

I felt my blood rushing to my face. Nadya laughed.

" That's why I'm asking you to come without Michael. Sergey won't be there, either. He'll only be back about midnight. We'll have dinner together. There'll be someone else."

" Michael won't be able to come, anyway," I said. " He's busy tonight. Some urgent work."

" So much the better. We'll have a cosy evening."

I told Michael that I was going " to see Chekhov ".

He frowned, but said nothing. He could not forbid me to go : it would have aroused too much talk, and he was afraid of that.

When I arrived at my sister's, Chekhov was not there. Nadya was sitting in her room in a dressing-gown, writing. And again she had that sly look on her face.

Then the maid came in and announced that Chekhov had arrived.

" Goodness, I shall have to dress! Go on, Lydia, and keep him company."

I went. He was standing in my brother-in-law's study.

" And what about your decision never to come to Petersburg again ? "

" I'm afraid I'm a very weak and undisciplined man. You look upset. Are you well ? Is anything the matter ? "

" I'm quite well, thank you, and everything's all right. Everything."

We sat down at the round table on which stood a tray with a piece of cheese and fruit. There was no bottle—yet.

" Yes, as you see, I'm in Petersburg again. And, you know, I'd like to write another play. . . ."

Nadya did not appear for a long time. In her absence we had time to discuss the theatre, the journals, and the editors to whom he strongly recommended me to go.

A chilled bottle of champagne was brought in.

" You recognise it ? " Nadya asked, pointing at the tray.

At first he looked puzzled.

" *A Boring Story*," Nadya reminded him.

He smiled and brushed back a strand of hair.

" Yes, yes. . . ."

Soon visitors appeared in the study.

" I'm sorry but Sergey won't be home before midnight," said Nadya.

The conversation became general.

" Haven't you seen Chekhov yet ? " I asked.

" Who ? " he asked in surprise.

" Chekhov! When did you arrive ? "

" I arrived yesterday," he replied, " and I happen to be Chekhov."

I felt awfully embarrassed.

" I mean Leykin! Leykin! " I cried. " I know you're Chekhov."

Everybody laughed, and Chekhov joined in and looked at me as I blushed to the roots of my hair.

" No, I haven't seen Leykin yet," he said. " You were asking about Leykin, weren't you? Quite sure? Not somebody else ? "

I, too, began to laugh. Suddenly I got frightened that I would not be able to stop and would burst out crying, and left the room.

When I returned, Chekhov got up and came up to me. We spoke for some time without sitting down and then, somehow without being aware of it ourselves, we went into the drawing-room.

" Tell me about your children," Chekhov said.

Oh, I did that willingly enough.

" Yes, children. . . ." said Chekhov reflectively. " Fine creatures. It's nice to have your—to have a family."

" You ought to get married."

" I ought to get married. But, you see, I'm not free. I may not be married, but I have a family : a mother, a sister, a younger brother. I have all sorts of duties."

" But are you happy ? " he asked suddenly.

This question took me by surprise and frightened me. I stopped, leaning against the grand-piano, and he stopped before me.

"Are you happy?" he insisted.

"But what is happiness?" I asked, at a loss how to answer his question. "I have a good husband and good children. But being fond of something doesn't mean being happy, does it? My mind is never at peace. I'm always worried. I'm entirely at the mercy of chance. It doesn't depend on me whether my children are in good health or alive, does it? And that's all I'm concerned about. That's all that matters to me. I seem to be gradually ceasing to exist. I've been caught in a trap and I can't set myself free. I often think with pain and regret that my life's finished. . . . I shall never be a writer or . . . I shan't be anything. All I can do is to make the best of things, to get used to everything, to cease to exist. Yes, to cease to exist, so that I shouldn't do anything that may harm my family by my desire for a better or happier life. I love my family. And soon, very soon, I shall give up the struggle. I shall cease to exist. Is that happiness?"

"That's the abnormal state of our family life," Chekhov said warmly. "It's the dependence and subjugation of women. It is something one must never accept, something one must fight against. It's just a survival from the past. . . . I understood very well what you were saying, though you did not tell me everything. You know, you ought to write up your life. Write it up sincerely and truthfully. It's important. It is necessary. You could do it in a way that would help not only you but also many others. You must do it and you must never cease to exist, but respect your personality and value your dignity as a human being. You're young and talented. . . . No, you mustn't let your family get you down. You will give it much more that way than if you just accept your present position and get reconciled to it. How can you say a thing like that ? "

He turned away and began to pace the room.

" I'm afraid my nerves are on edge today. Of course I exaggerated a lot. . . ."

" If I'd married," Chekhov said thoughtfully, " I'd have proposed to my wife. . . . You know, I'd have proposed to her that we should not live together. So that there shouldn't be all that laxity of behaviour—all that undignified familiarity and—and all that abominable unceremoniousness."

Suddenly a maid came in and told me—

" You're urgently wanted at home, ma'am."

" What's happened ? " I cried, startled.

" Lyovushka seems to have been taken ill. Anyuta has been sent for you."

" Dear Mr. Chekhov, please tell Nadya. I'd rather not go in there. Please explain. Good-bye."

I was trembling all over.

He took me by the hand.

" You mustn't worry. I don't expect there's anything wrong. It happens with children. Calm yourself, please."

He came down the stairs with me.

" Let me know tomorrow how your little boy is. I'll be waiting for news here. Don't forget to take a glass of wine when you reach home."

Anyuta was waiting for me in the hall. She looked very calm.

" What's the matter with Lyova ? "

" I don't know, ma'am. He woke up and asked for some water. He didn't complain of anything. Master came in. . . ."

Michael himself opened the door for me.

"It's nothing, nothing," he greeted me, looking rather sheepish. "He's gone to sleep again and I don't think he has a temperature. I was worried about him without you. When you're out I don't know what to do. He asked for some water. I don't know why. Does he drink water at night? He also asked about you: where's mummy? You see, mother, we're all lost without you."

He went with me to the nursery. Lyova was peacefully asleep. He had no temperature at all.

Michael drew me to him and would not let me go.

"You're my fairy godmother. When you're at home I'm not worried. I know everything's all right."

I remembered how he had hurled his plate of fritters on the floor at dinner because they were not in his opinion crisp and puffy enough. "They're only good to throw to dogs!"

"But don't you realise how you've frightened me?"

"I'm sorry, darling. Angry? How stern you are with me! Keep me under your thumb, do you? But I can't live without you. I'm sorry. Let's talk it over. You see, you were out the whole evening. . . ."

But I knew now. I knew for the first time, without a doubt, definitely, clearly. I knew that I was in love with Chekhov.

FIVE

IT WAS shrove-tide. One of those rare Petersburg shrove-tides—no thaw, no rain, no fog. Soft, white, tender.

Michael had gone to the Caucasus, and everything was quiet and peaceful at home.

The Leykins were giving a party on Friday and I too had been invited. They lived in their own house in the Petersburg suburb.

First I went to the theatre, to the Italian opera, I believe, where I had a season ticket. I arrived at the Leykins' rather late. Mrs. Leykin met me in the hall, all dressed up, radiant, and, as always, very pleased to see me.

"I was afraid you wouldn't come," she said loudly. "It would have been such a pity. You're expected," she whispered to me, but in such a loud voice that it was only the quality of the voice that had changed but not its strength.

"Have I kept someone waiting? Whom? What?"

" They're waiting for you . . ."

" Pancakes ? Have you got pancakes ? "

" Of course! Of course we have pancakes! " she burst out laughing and dragged me by the hand to her husband's study.

There were lots of people there. Leykin got up and limped towards me.

" You're very late. Oh, I see, you were at the theatre. And your husband ? In the Caucasus ? I believe you know everybody. Potapenko, Albov, Gruzinsky, Barantsevich. . . ."

" Don't protract the agony! " shouted Mrs. Leykin and burst out laughing.

There remained only one more visitor whose name Leykin did not mention. He got up from the sofa and remained standing there. I turned round to him.

" The pancake! " cried Mrs. Leykin. " Here's your pancake! "

We shook hands in silence.

" What are you talking about, my dear ? " Leykin addressed his wife, looking perplexed. " Why's Chekhov a pancake ? "

They all resumed their seats.

" I was just saying," Leykin resumed the interrupted conversation, addressing himself to me, " I was just telling him " —he motioned towards Chekhov—" that it was a great pity he did not consult me when he was writing his last story. Not that I'm criticising it in any way. Heavens, no! He's written it beautifully, but I'd have written it differently. And it would have been much better. You remember in my story—from the basement only walking feet are seen : a pair of old galoshes shuffle by, a pair of ladies' shoes walk mincingly across, a pair of broken children's boots run past. New. Interesting. One must know how to construct a story. I'd have done it differently."

56

Chekhov smiled.

"Your basement was a great success," said one of the visitors.

And all at once a whole chorus of voices began to praise our host's story. Other stories of his were mentioned. People laughed. Praised their humour. But I remembered Nadya's words: "You know, he doesn't suspect his stories are humorous. He thinks he's writing serious stuff. He takes his models from life. Writes up his own and his wife's relations. Even himself. The result is excruciatingly funny, but he believes it's serious. He never sees how funny it is. I wonder why he writes. Why isn't he a shopkeeper? An odd talent."

Soon we were asked to go in to supper. There was a lot of everything: snacks, food, vodka, wines, but most of all noise. Our host alone sat with a grave expression on his face, as though crushed under the weight of his merits both as a literary man, a town councillor, and a hospitable houseowner. He kept praising the pancakes and comparing everything with Moscow.

"Have you ever tasted such whitefish in Moscow, my dear Chekhov? How deliciously tender and juicy! It's not white-fish: it's butter! Now, I know how proud you in Moscow are of your sucking pigs, but just try this one. As good as yours, I'll be bound. I had some veal at dinner at Khudekov's the other day. A pity he isn't here tonight. I'd have asked him to sample this bit of veal here. You see, you have to choose everything yourself, and you have to know what's what. I have real veal, and he's a millionaire!"

Chekhov was in high spirits. He did not laugh loud (he never laughed loud), nor did he raise his voice, but he kept everyone amused by his unexpected remarks. He suddenly began to express his admiration for the fat epaulettes of some army officer, assuring everybody that if he had such epaulettes he'd be the happiest man on earth.

" How the women would have loved me! They would have fallen in love with me by the score! I'm sure of it."

When we rose from the table, he said, " I'd like to see you home. All right ? "

We went out of the house in a crowd. The sledges were drawn up along the pavement, and some of them were already moving off with their fares. Afraid that they would be all taken, I asked Chekhov to hurry up. He at once went up to a sledge, sat down in it, and shouted to me, " Come on, everything's all right! "

I went up. Chekhov, however, had sat down at the side of the pavement so that I had to go round the sledge before I could get into it. I was wearing a cloak and my hands were not free, particularly as under my cloak I had to hold the train of my dress, my handbag, and my opera-glasses. My feet sank in the snow and I found it very difficult to get into the sledge without any assistance.

" What a cavalier! " shouted Potapenko as he moved off in his sledge.

Somehow or other, sideways, I scrambled into the sledge. Someone tucked the hem of my cloak into the sledge and fastened its cover. We drove off.

" What was it he shouted about a cavalier ? " asked Chekhov. " Did he mean me ? Good Lord, what sort of cavalier am I ? I'm a doctor. And, anyway, what was it I did wrong as a cavalier ? "

" Why, no one behaves like that. A lady must be helped into a sledge first, and the gentleman must make sure that she's comfortable before he gets into it himself, and he must make the best of what room there is left for him."

"I hate your sententious tone," said Chekhov. "When you're grumbling you look just like an old woman. Oh, if only I had a pair of epaulettes! . . ."

"What? Your epaulettes again?"

"Oh, well, angry again, and grumbling. And all because I didn't carry your train."

"Look here, doctor, I'm trying my best to prevent myself from being flung out of the sledge and you keep on prodding me with your elbow. I'm sure I'll be thrown out in a minute."

"You've got a horrid character. But if I had a pair of epaulettes. . . ."

He then started putting on his gloves. He had a pair of enormous leather gloves.

"Show me your gloves, please. Give them to me. What are they made of? Frieze?"

"No, they're fur gloves. Here!"

"Where did you get such lovely gloves?"

"At a factory near Serpukhov. Jealous?"

I put them on under my cloak and said, "Not at all. They are mine."

The driver was already crossing the bridge.

"Where to, sir?"

"Ertel Lane," I cried, giving Suvorin's address where Chekhov was staying.

"No, why? Nikolayevskaya Street."

"No, Ertel Lane. I'll see you home, then I'll make myself comfortable in the sledge and drive home."

"And I'll run after you in the sledge like a dog in deep snow, and without my gloves, too. Driver, Nikolayevskaya!"

The driver drew in the reins, and the sledge stopped.

"You'd better make up your mind, sir. . . . Where am I to go?"

We drove to Nikolayevskaya Street. I gave him back his gloves, and Chekhov began to praise them in imitation of Leykin.

" I'm sure Khudekov hasn't got such gloves, and yet he is a millionaire. No, ma'am. You have to go to the factory yourself. To Serpukhov. And you must know what's what. . . . Well, are you going to write a novel ? Do. And remember a woman must write just as she embroiders. Write a lot and in detail. Write and cut. Write and cut."

" Till there's nothing left ? "

" You've got a horrid character. I find it difficult to talk to you. No. Write, I implore you. Write, but nothing fictitious or fantastic. Just life as it is. Will you write ? "

" I will, but I'm going to write fiction. This is what I'd like to write. Listen. The love story of an unknown man. Understand ? You don't know him, but he's in love with you. And you always feel it. You're always surrounded by someone's loving care. You know that someone is always anxious to make you happy. You receive such clever, such delightful letters, full of passion, and every minute of your life you are conscious of someone's solicitude for you. See what I mean? And you get used to it, you are already waiting for something to happen, you are afraid to lose something. The man you don't know is already dear to you, and you want to know him. And then what do you discover ? What do you find out ? Don't you think it's interesting ? "

" I don't. Not a bit interesting, my dear child," said Chekhov quickly, and the quickness and firmness with which he had said it and the " my dear child " amused me so much that I burst out laughing, and I went on laughing a long time.

" Why—my dear child ? "

We were getting near Nikolayevskaya Street.

" Will you be long here ? " I asked.

" I'd like to stay another week. Couldn't we see each other more often ? Every day ? All right ? "

" Come and see me tomorrow evening," I proposed before I knew myself what I was saying.

Chekhov looked surprised.

" At your place ? "

For some reason neither of us said anything for some time.

" Do you expect many visitors ? " Chekhov asked.

" On the contrary, none at all. Michael has gone to the Caucasus. Nadya never comes to see me in the evening. We shall be alone and we'll be able to talk and talk. . . ."

" I'll do my best to persuade you to write a novel. You really must."

" So you'll come ? "

" If I'm not dragged off somewhere else. I'm staying with Suvorin, and I'm afraid I'm not my own master."

" I'll wait for you all the same. About nine."

We arrived, and I got out and rang the doorbell.

The sledge with Chekhov drove off and began to turn round, describing a huge circle on the wide, deserted street. We kept talking to one another.

" I will come," Chekhov was saying in his beautiful low voice, which sounded so lovely in the stillness of the wide street and in the soft wintry air. " I want to persuade you to write a novel. All about how you were in love with an army officer."

" Who told you that ? "

" You did. A long time ago. Remember ? You're not going to deny it, are you ? "

The porter was opening the door with his overcoat thrown over his shoulders.

" Good-bye till tomorrow."

" Yes, till tomorrow. And you won't be cross with me, will you ? You'll try to be kind, very kind. A woman must always be gentle and kind."

Little did I know what was in store for me.

SIX

AT LAST the evening came.

After nine o'clock I began waiting for him.

I had prepared a little cold supper, vodka, wine, beer, fruit. In the dining-room the table was laid for tea. I had planned it all very carefully : first I'd take him to the nursery. Make him a little jealous. The children would not be asleep yet. They would be just going to bed. They were particularly sweet just then. It was their happiest time. Then we would go into the dining-room and have tea. Next we would move into the study where it was much cosier than in the drawing-room. How much we had to say to each other!

We should have supper later. I dared not buy champagne. I couldn't help feeling that that would have been almost an insult to Michael. And, besides, I had already spent much more than I should have. (I remember I did not pay my account at the chandler's : they could wait.)

At half-past nine the doorbell rang. My hand pressed to my heart, I waited a little for Masha to open the front-door. I heard her go to the door, open it, and say something to the visitor. Then I, too, went out into the entrance hall and froze with horror. There were two visitors : a man and a woman, and they were taking off their coats. That meant that there was no mistake : they intended to stay the whole evening. And the frightful thing was that they were friends of Michael's whom I detested so much that he had always to drag me to visit them by main force. I didn't mind him so much. It was her I simply could not stand. Both were mathematicians. They taught somewhere, and in their flat they had two writing-desks which were placed side by side, and this for some reason made me feel furious. Both of them were very busy and, thank goodness, came to see us very rarely. And they would come just on that evening.

" Yes, it's us, it's us! " cried Vera. " And Michael's away in the Caucasus ? Ha-ha-ha! "

She had a nasty habit of shrieking with laughter on any and every occasion. Whenever she said something, she shrieked with laughter. How on earth did she teach, I wondered. I remember her telling me once about the death of her only child and simply roaring with laughter at the same time.

And now that laughter resounded all over the flat. I naturally had to invite them into the drawing-room. The large lamp was burning dimly and the whole atmosphere of the room was pervaded by a feeling of gentle sadness. But Vera roared at the top of her voice. She was telling me how a girl she knew had had a nervous breakdown because her fiancé had died or had jilted her and how she had advised her to solve mathematical problems. She started doing it and got well, forgot all about her unhappy love affair, was now studying mathematics intensively, and was as merry as a cricket.

" Why don't you try it ? " she asked me. " Solving problems disciplines your mind, keeps you from dreaming, and strengthens your character. Make your children do sums. You'll see how useful it will be for them. Ha-ha-ha! "

At ten Masha announced that tea was served.

I gave a start and rushed into the dining-room. It was as I feared. My whole supper was on the table. Wine, fruit, and all.

" My goodness, look at the spread! " I heard Vera scream behind my back. " Were you expecting visitors ? Peter, what a good thing we had our dinner so early. How lovely! Ha-ha-ha! But why ? "

They began to eat. Both seemed to enjoy the food very much. I did what was expected of me. Asked them to help themselves to everything.

" What delicious sauce! Your cook, isn't it ? Yourself ? No, it can't be! And Michael told me that you didn't like cooking. Too busy with writing. Fiction, poetry."

And here she burst out into such a roar of laughter that she nearly choked herself.

It was half-past ten by our large dining-room clock. It was clear that Chekhov would not be coming, and I could not help feeling glad.

Suddenly the doorbell rang, and I heard Chekhov's voice. He was asking Masha about something.

" What's the matter ? " Vera cried. " Peter, quick. A glass of water! Lydia's going to faint! "

" No, thank you," I said weakly, " I—I'm quite all right. What made you think I was going to faint ? "

" But you're as white as a sheet. And now you've gone red in the face. . . ."

Chekhov came in and I introduced them to one another.
What a roar of laughter!

" What ? Chekhov ? And Lydia didn't warn us that she was expecting such a visitor ? What a lucky chance! Now you'll be able to answer the questions I ask myself every time I read your stories. You simply must answer me."

She pounced on Chekhov like a lynx on an inoffensive deer. She drove her teeth into him and began to tear him to pieces. She screamed. She shrieked with laughter. She accused him of wasting his genius on writing silly little tales, of always going round and about a subject, of not solving problems, of not giving people some great ideal to live for. Everything he wrote was so vague. Nothing exact. No mathematical precision. No mathematical precision. None at all. Ha-ha-ha!

Chekhov looked at me in dismay a few times. Suddenly he asked me,

" Do you smoke ? "

Vera fell silent for a moment, blinking in surprise. I, too, was rather taken aback.

" No. . . ."

" I thought you had a cigarette."

" I have nothing! " and I showed him my hands.

" You mustn't smoke."

Vera began shouting again, jumping up and down on her chair and rending the air with her screams which seemed to deprive me of breath. I felt positively stifled.

Chekhov defended himself weakly, unwillingly. He spoke in monosyllables. He sat over his glass of tea without raising his eyes.

But suddenly Peter got up and said to his wife, " Vera, it's time we went home."

" Home ? " she cried. " No, Peter, I shan't have another

chance of telling Mr. Chekhov what he should be told. He must realise that it is his duty as a writer . . ."

And off she went again. I drew comfort from the fact that her husband did not resume his seat but remained on his feet. He insisted that it was time they went, and of course I did not raise any objections. I was afraid, though, that he would not be able to prevail on his wife who seemed to have completely lost control of herself in her desire to do her duty and set Chekhov on the right path. Luckily, however, he did prevail in the end. She hurled herself on Chekhov for the last time, started shaking and pressing his hand, roaring into his ears that he was a great, great genius and that she believed in him and expected a lot from him. At last her shouts were transferred to the hall, and then to the stairs, her roars of laughter shaking the whole floor of the building. The door slammed and Chekhov and I, utterly exhausted, went into the study.

" You look jaded," said Chekhov. " I'd better go. Your visitors have tired you."

I don't know what was the matter with me. I could hardly utter a word.

" Please, stay! Please. . . ."

" By the way, where are those things you promised to let me have ? The papers with your stories and your manuscript."

I had already prepared it all and I handed him the packet.

" Why don't you want me to take your manuscript to Goltsev ? To *Russian Thought*."

" Because if they accept it, it will not be on its merits, but because of your recommendation."

" But I should never dream of recommending it if it had no merit. Don't you believe me ? "

" It isn't that I don't believe you, but, I'm afraid, very often I can't understand your criticism at all. ' Your story is all right. Very good, as a matter of fact. But Dunya (the heroine of my story) should have been a man. Make her an army officer or something of the kind. And the hero (my hero was a student who was in love with Dunya) must be a clerk in an inland revenue office.' You see, I remember your criticism by heart. But what kind of love story can there be between an army officer and a clerk of the inland revenue ? And if there ought not to be any love story at all, then what is there so good, and so very good even, about my story ? "

" All right, you should have left everything as it was. I assure you, it was a good story. I wrote you that your style is excellent and that if I'd been an editor, I'd have paid you at least two hundred per sheet. But you don't go where I send you. You seem to go to all sorts of queer places. Why did you send your story to *The Patriot* ? Krivenko is an excellent fellow, but that's neither here nor there. Do you know what they've nicknamed his paper ? The corpse of an honest man. A real bull's-eye. And you'll never bring this corpse to life. Why did you go there ? "

" Oh, that's nothing," I replied listlessly. " You don't know where I've been. I've been to Burenin."*

Chekhov jumped up from his chair. Even the skirts of his coat flew up.

" What fool sent you to that scoundrel ? " he asked sternly, without raising his voice but frowning so angrily that I could not help feeling surprised.

" Yes, I did go to him," I confirmed. " He told me that if I brought him my stories myself . . . You understand ? If I

---

* Viktor Burenin, a critic on the staff of Suvorin's reactionary paper *Novoye Vremya* (New Time).

went to him and by myself ... . then he would publish them."

I felt sorry almost as soon as I had said it. It was not necessary, and it was silly. I was simply pleased that Chekhov was angry and I tried to create a bigger impression. That's what is known as flirting.

" Of course I went away with my manuscript and I shall never go there again," I added.

" Please, do believe me a little. Do as I tell you and do not run the risk of finding yourself in an awkward situation. There are many more good people than bad ones. I wish I could protect you from the bad."

He calmed down, and I went to the dining-room for the wine. Besides, it was time he had something to eat. But—what miserable remnants of a meal Vera and Peter had left! I collected what I could and put it on Michael's writing desk. My packet with the manuscripts I put down on the little round table by the window.

" I'd rather not have that," said Chekhov, and I got the impression that he had said it with a shudder of disgust. He took the bottle of wine, put it down, and poured himself out a glass of beer. I felt hurt and also ashamed. Some reception I prepared for him, I must say.

" You ought to go to bed," said Chekhov. " Your visitors have tired you. You're not the same today as you were before. You look indifferent and listless, and you'll be glad when I'm gone. Yes, before. . . . Remember our first meetings ? And do you know—do you know that I was deeply in love with you ? Seriously in love with you ? Yes, I loved you. It seemed to me that there was not another woman in the world I could love like that. You were beautiful and sweet and there was such freshness in your youth, such dazzling charm. I loved you and

I thought only of you. And when I met you again after our long separation it seemed to me that you were more beautiful than ever, that you were quite a different person, quite a new person, and that I must get to know you again and love you even more—in a new way. And that it would be even harder to leave you. . . ."

He sat on the sofa with his head thrown back against it. I was sitting on a chair opposite him. He spoke quietly, his wonderful low voice filling the room, and his face was stern and his eyes were cold and remorseless.

" Did you know that ? "

I had the impression that he was angry with me and that he was reproaching me for having deceived him, for having changed, for having lost my looks, for being listless and indifferent, and no longer desirable now.

" It's a nightmare! " the thought flashed through my mind.

" I loved you," Chekhov went on, almost furiously now, and he bent over, staring angrily at my face. " But I knew that you were not like many other women, and that the love one can feel for you must be pure and sacred and must last all one's life. I was afraid to touch you so as not to offend. Did you know that ? "

He took my hand and almost immediately relinquished it with, as it seemed to me, disgust.

" Oh, what a cold hand! "

And he got up at once and looked at the clock.

" Half-past one. I shall still have time to have supper and discuss things with Suvorin. You'd better go to bed at once. At once."

His eyes were searching for something on the table, on the sofa.

70

" I believe I promised to see you tomorrow, but I'm afraid I shan't have time. I shall be leaving for Moscow tomorrow. This means that we shan't see each other again."

He looked round the room again and then went up to the little table by the window and took the parcel with the manuscripts. I was sitting as though dead, without moving.

My ears rang, thoughts rushed through my head, but I could not get hold of any one of them. They seemed to be beyond my grasp, and I could not understand anything. I couldn't say anything, either. Oh, what was going on in my head? How frightful it all was.

I dragged myself out of the chair and went to see him to the door.

" So we shan't see each other again," he repeated.

I made no reply, but just shook his hand listlessly.

We lived on the fourth floor. The stairs were brightly lit. I stood on the landing and watched him run downstairs. When he reached the third floor, I called to him—

" Anton Pavlovich! "

He stopped, raised his head, waited a minute, and then started running down the stairs again.

I said nothing.

SEVEN

Next day I received by messenger a parcel with a book, my manuscripts, and a letter. The book was his latest collection of short stories, which had only just come out, with a cold inscription: "To L. A. Avilova from the author." The letter was as follows :

" 15th February 1895. St. Petersburg.
" In spite of the fact that Marconi and Battistini were singing in the next room, I read both your stories with great attention. *Power* is a delightful story, but I can't help thinking that it would be improved if you made your hero simply a landowner instead of the head of a rural council. As for *Birthday*, it is not, I'm afraid, a story at all, but just a thing, and a clumsy thing at that. You have piled up a whole mountain of details, and this mountain has obscured the sun. You ought to make it either into a long short story, about four folio

73

sheets, or a very short story, beginning with the episode when the old nobleman is carried into the house.

"To sum up: you are a talented woman, but you have grown heavy, or, to put it vulgarly, you have grown stale and you already belong to the category of stale authors. Your style is precious, like the style of very old writers. . . . The surface of the snow is a very awkward expression. Then one comes across such curious bits as ' Nikifor detached himself from the gatepost ', or ' he detached himself from a wall '.

"Write a novel. Spend a whole year on it and another six months in abridging it, and then publish it. You don't seem to take enough trouble with your work, and a woman writer ought not to write but to embroider on paper so that her work ought to be slow and painstaking. Forgive me these exhortations of mine. Sometimes one cannot help feeling like being a little pompous and reading a lecture. I stayed for another day here, or rather was forced to stay, but I'm leaving for certain tomorrow.

"I wish you all the best. Yours sincerely,

Chekhov."*

Chekhov had told me off properly: " grown heavy and stale." He was cross with me. But I had already had time to think things over, and though I did not come to any definite

* The same day, probably in reply to a letter from her, Chekhov wrote Lydia a second (unpublished) letter, which he sent with the book mentioned in the memoirs.

" Dear Lydia Alexeyevna,

" You are wrong. I was not horribly bored at your place, but just a little depressed because I could see from the expression on your face that you were sick and tired of your visitors. I should have liked to have dinner with you, but you did not repeat your invitation yesterday and I concluded once more that you were tired of visitors.

" I did not see Burenin today and I don't think I shall be seeing him because I intend to leave for home tomorrow. I am sending you my book and a thousand of good wishes and blessings. Write a novel.

" Yours sincerely,

Chekhov."

74

conclusion, I did, or so it seemed to me, begin to reason logically. Not that this logic did me any good. The truth is I hated to act in accordance with it. But should not one's reason triumph over one's feelings? Think of the silly things I had already done because of these very feelings! I had invited Chekhov to come and see me when Michael was out of town. And what could Chekhov have thought of it? That I had deliberately arranged to be alone with him. What other conclusion could he possibly have drawn?

I don't know how it happened, but a sudden gale seemed to have swept away all my arguments. And this gale was my faith, my love, and my great sorrow.

" I loved you and I thought only of you. . . ."

Having spent another two anxious days in trying to come to a decision, I at last made up my mind. I went to a jeweller's and ordered a pendant for a watch-chain in the form of a book. I had it engraved on one side : " Short Stories by Chekhov," and on the other, " Page 267, lines 6 and 7."

If Chekhov had looked up those lines in his book, he would have read : " If you ever want my life, come and take it."

When the pendant was ready, I sent it to my brother in Moscow, and he took it to the office of *Russian Thought* and handed it to Goltsev with a request to send it on to Chekhov.

I did it out of sheer despair. I did not send any message with the pendant, but had it engraved, so that there should be no direct confession and that some doubt should still be left in his mind, while also leaving myself a way of retreat if that should be necessary. I could not possibly have given him all my life! For it would have meant sacrificing four lives at once : mine and my three children's. But would Michael have given me my children ? And could Chekhov have taken them ?

.   .   .   .   .

There could be no doubt that Chekhov received my present. I was anxiously waiting for something to happen. I spent many days in a state of agitation and alarm. One day I expected him to come and another day I expected a letter from him and tried to think what it would contain. I fancied he would just give me a good talking to, and I was already preparing a correspondingly biting reply; or I would imagine that his letter would just contain a few casual lines, a kind of gratuity, a gracious permission to keep up our acquaintance and our correspondence.

But time passed and there was neither Chekhov nor any letter from him. There was nothing.

Oh, how sick I got of analysing my own thoughts! Repeating to myself everything Chekhov had said to me, every word of his, which I remembered by heart and which always brought Chekhov's face and voice so vividly to my mind.

One thing I knew for certain: nothing could be more understandable, natural, and even irrevocable than the fact that I was in love with Chekhov. I couldn't help admiring not only his genius, but also himself, everything he said, his thoughts, his views. . . .

Once he said to me : " You possess an inborn, an instinctive moral sense. That means a lot." He had said it in this connection : an argument arose whether it was right that a mistake in the choice of a husband or a wife should be allowed to ruin the lives of two people. Some argued that there could be no question of right or wrong and that if the church had sanctified the marriage, it must remain inviolate. Others warmly protested against such a view, bringing all sorts of arguments to prove that it was wrong. Chekhov was silent, then he asked me quietly, " And what's your opinion ? " I said. " One has first to be sure whether it is worth it." " I don't understand,"

Chekhov said. " What is worth it ? " " Whether the new feeling is worth all the sacrifices, for there must be sacrifices. First of all, there are the children. One has to think of those who would suffer from such a step, and not of oneself. One should have no pity for oneself. Then it will be clear whether it is worth it or not."

Afterwards, a long time afterwards, I remembered this conversation and I could not help feeling that it had been of great importance. It was then that Chekhov told me, " You possess an instinctive moral sense. . . . That means a lot."

But was that enough that he should be able to love ? He!

There could be no doubt that Chekhov had received my pendant, but he never replied, and even our correspondence came to an end. I had to make up my mind to live without him.

EIGHT

IT WAS shrove-tide again. In the evening I was sitting in Michael's study, reading. My brother, who had arrived from Moscow, was in the drawing-room playing the piano. My husband was sitting at his desk, writing something. Suddenly the lid of the piano came down with a crash, and my brother Alexey came into the room.

"I'm bored stiff!" he cried. "What the hell have I come to Petersburg for? Let's go somewhere!"

Michael glanced at the clock.

"Where do you want to go to at this hour of the night? You're mad."

"It's not twelve o'clock yet. Late, indeed! Come on, bestir yourself!"

He grasped my hand and began pulling me up.

"But where shall we go?" I protested weakly.

" There's a mask ball at Suvorin's theatre tonight," said Alexey after glancing through the paper. " Excellent! "

" But the fancy dress ? Or domino ? "

" Nonsense! We'll find something! Come on, quick! "

He pulled me out of the chair and rushed me to my bedroom.

" Get dressed, and I——"

Michael refused point blank to come with us.

While we were putting on our overcoats in the hall, he shouted to us :

" Madmen! Gadabouts! "

" Shut up, you ministerial rat! " Alexey replied.

We took a sledge and drove to Vladimirskaya Street where there was a little fancy-dress shop. But, alas, it was closed.

" Doesn't mean a thing! " said Alexey, pounding on the door of the shop.

" Stop it! " I shouted to him from the sledge. " What are you doing ? You'll get yourself into trouble : there's a policeman coming! "

" That's splendid! " said my brother without seeming in the least put out.

When the policeman came, Alexey said something quietly to him and it looked to me as if he had pressed his hand. The policeman immediately began to knock on the door himself, and though he knocked much more quietly, the door opened at once and the owner of the shop, an old woman in a petticoat and a night jacket, appeared on the threshold. The policeman said something to her, saluted Alexey, and even helped me out of the sledge.

We chose our costumes by the light of a candle. There was not much to choose from : everything had already been taken. All I could find was a black domino. It was a little too short for me, but I had to make the best of it.

In a few more minutes we drove up to the entrance of the theatre.

"Don't leave me alone," I said to my brother. "I'm terrified."

The auditorium of the theatre looked as though it were a scene in a nightmare. It was tightly packed with people, and I could only move together with the crowd in one direction. I felt in my handbag for the two nuts that had been left there after a game of lotto with my children and put them into my mouth to make sure my voice would not reveal my identity if I happened to meet some people I knew.

"Don't choke!" my brother warned me, and suddenly almost shouted, "Look to your right!"

To the right stood Chekhov. Screwing up his eyes, he gazed somewhere far away over the heads of the people.

"Now of course I can go, can't I?" said Alexey, and immediately vanished.

I went up to Chekhov.

"Hullo, darling," I said. "I'm so glad to see you."

"You don't know me, mask," he replied, scrutinising me closely.

I trembled with excitement and surprise. Had he noticed it? Without uttering a word, he took my arm, put his arm through it, and led me round in the circle. Nemirovich-Danchenko darted past us.

"Oh-oh-oh!" he shouted to Chekhov. "So you've already picked someone up!"

Chekhov bent over to me and said softly:

"If anyone calls you by your name, don't turn round. Don't give yourself away!"

"No one knows me here," I squeaked in reply.

Nemirovich-Danchenko somehow managed to circle round

and round us and every time he shouted to Chekhov:
" Oh-oh-oh! "

" He couldn't have recognised you, could he ? " Chekhov
asked anxiously. " Don't turn round. Would you like a drink?
Let's go to a box and have a glass of champagne."

We made our way out of the crowd with difficulty, went up
the stairs to the boxes, and found ourselves in an empty
corridor.

" Ah, that's perfect! " said Chekhov. " I was afraid
Nemirovich would call you by your name and you would give
yourself away."

" But do you know who I am ? Well, who am I ? Who ?
Tell me! "

I snatched my arm away from him and stopped. He smiled.

" You know my play will be on soon, don't you ? " he
asked me without answering my question.

" Yes, I know. *The Seagull.*"

" *The Seagull.* Will you be at the first night ? "

" I will. I promise."

" Well, listen very carefully. I will reply to you from the
stage. Only remember, listen carefully. Don't forget."

He again took my arm and pressed it to himself.

" What will you reply to ? "

" I'll give you my reply to many things. Only follow the
play carefully and remember everything."

We went into an empty box. There were bottles and glasses
on a table.

" It's Suvorin's box. Let's sit down. Let's clink glasses."

He began to fill the glasses.

" I don't understand," I said. " You're not making fun of
me, darling, are you ? How can you say something to me from
the stage ? And how am I to know which words are meant for

me ? Besides, you don't know who I am. Do you ? Do you ? "

" You'll understand. . . . Sit down. Have a drink, please."

" It's hot! "

I went up to the looking-glass.

" Want to powder your nose ? All right, I shan't look. Take off your mask."

He sat down with his back to me. I watched him in the glass. He did not move, but I did not take off my mask.

Then we sat down and drank.

" Do you like the title—The Seagull ? "

" Very much."

" The Seagull. It has such a desolate cry. When it cries one can't help thinking of something sad."

" And why are you so sad tonight ? " I asked. " You always look over the heads of the people as though you didn't care for anyone, as though you were too bored to look at people."

He smiled.

" You are wrong, mask," he said. " I'm not bored tonight."

I returned to the subject of *The Seagull*.

" How can you possibly tell me something from the stage ? If you had known who I was, I would have thought that you had put me into your play. . . ."

" No, no! "

" Well, in that case I don't understand. I'm sure I shall never be able to understand! Particularly as most probably you'll not reply to me at all, but to the woman you are taking me for."

" Let's go down," Chekhov proposed. " I shouldn't like anyone to find us here."

We went back to the auditorium. At first we walked round, then we sat down.

" Tell me something," Chekhov said. " Tell me about yourself. Tell me about your love affair."

" What love affair ? It's you who are writing love stories, not me."

" I don't mean a fictitious one. A real one. You must have been in love with someone."

" I don't know."

Crowds of people were moving past us, the women rustling their dresses and everybody making a noise. Not the usual well-dressed crowd, but a kind of fairy-tale crowd, a crowd in a dream. Instead of women's faces, black and coloured masks with narrow slits for the eyes. Here and there animal faces protruded from under the raised hoods of the men's dominoes, and their boiled shirts dazzled the eye. And over it all came the intoxicating strains of the orchestra playing waltzes and passionate airs. My head was beginning to swim a little, my nerves were on edge, my heart beat fast and now and then seemed to stop beating altogether. I pressed my shoulder against Chekhov's shoulder and gazed closely into his eyes.

" I loved you," I said to him. " You, you. . . ."

" You're flirting, mask," he said. " And, besides, you're contradicting yourself : you just told me I didn't know you."

" No, I'm not contradicting myself. Maybe it wasn't love, but there was not an hour I didn't think of you. And when I was with you, I did not want to leave you. I was so happy that I could not bear it. Don't you believe me ? Oh, my dear! "

He brushed back a strand of hair and raised his eyes to the ceiling.

" Don't you believe me ? Answer me."

" I don't know you, mask."

" You may not know me, but all the same you are taking me for someone. You said you'd give me your reply from the stage."

" I said it just in case. If you're not the woman I wanted to say it to, then it doesn't matter. You won't understand anything then."

" And who did you want to tell it to ? "

He turned round to me :

" To you! "

" Then why did you say you didn't know me ? "

" I know you're an actress and you're acting very well now."

" And is it the actress who must be very, very attentive and follow everything carefully? "

" You! "

He smiled again and inclined his head towards me.

" Pay attention and follow everything carefully. But you did not finish telling me your love story. Go on, I'm listening."

" It's a boring love story and it has an unhappy ending."

" An unhappy ending ? "

" I told you I did not know for certain whether I was in love or not. Is it love when you're always fighting against it, when you're always trying to drive it away, when you're always, always hoping that you're no longer in love, that you're getting over it, and that, at last, you have got over it ? Is that love ? "

" If there hadn't been any love," he said quickly, " there wouldn't have been any fight."

" Oh, so you do believe me! "

" I don't know you, mask."

He took my arm and got up.

" There are lots of prying eyes here. Do you want another drink ? I do."

We went up to the box again, and after Chekhov had made sure that there was no one there, we sat down.

There were two almost full bottles on the table, and we began talking happily about anything that came into our heads. He insisted that I was an actress and that he had seen me in tragic parts. I began to tease him with Yavorskaya.

" Are you still in love with her, you unhappy wretch ? "

" Do you really think I'm going to tell you ? "

" Why shouldn't you tell me ? "

" Because you're probably Yavorskaya yourself."

" Are you sure ? "

" Quite sure."

" You should have told me that before. I'd have taken off my mask."

" Well, take it off ! "

" No, it's too late now. It's time I went home."

We looked down. The crowd had thinned perceptibly. I saw Alexey who was screwing up his eyes in an effort to find me. Yes, he was looking for me. Laughing, we quickly went downstairs and knocked against Suvorin and Co.

" My dear Chekhov," he exclaimed, " we were looking all over the place for you. . . ."

I quickly pressed Chekhov's hand and rushed up to Alexey.

" Happy? " he asked.

" Happy and a little drunk. And you ? "

" I, too, am happy, but as sober as a judge."

On the way back home and in bed at home I could not help asking myself whether Chekhov really thought I was Yavorskaya and whether his reply from the stage was meant for her.

Michael and I were confirmed first-nighters and I thought that this time, too, he would come with me, but he gave me only one ticket.

" Here you are, you Chekhov-fiend! Cost me a lot of trouble to get it, and it isn't for the stalls, either. Dress circle."

" And what about you? "

" I have a meeting. And, to tell you the truth, I don't think I shall miss much."

I went alone and, to tell the truth, I too was very glad to be alone. I did not, of course, breathe a word to anyone about expecting a reply from the stage, not even to Alexey, but I could not conceal my excitement. I had been waiting a long time for this day, and all the time I had been thinking of all sorts of things. Had Chekhov recognised me or had he taken me for someone else ? He said he was " quite sure " I was Yavorskaya. I decided that it could not be. He was pulling my leg. Neither in my figure nor in my manner of speaking did I in any way resemble Yavorskaya. But he must have known hundreds of other women!

Incidentally, I remembered that it was for the second time in my life that I had been to a mask ball. The first time I had gone with Michael and a whole crowd of his friends. I did my best to flirt, but a great many men I did not know tried to persuade me to have supper with them and go for a ride in a *troika*. I was terrified and took to my heels. I did not feel at all happy, but hated every moment of it, and I should never have gone arm in arm with anyone, nor would I have accepted an invitation to have a drink. With Chekhov I immediately consented to go to an empty box, and for some reason I was not even surprised that he behaved himself all the time as though he were not at a mask ball but at the house of some friends. He seemed anxious to protect me from " prying eyes " and he was afraid that I might give myself away. And I seemed to have taken it for granted that it could not possibly have been otherwise. Once I was with Chekhov all that was quite natural, whoever I was. His respect for women and his sense of personal dignity and honour was the best guarantee any woman could wish to have against any unprovoked annoyance.

But who did he want to give his reply to from the stage?

" You! " he had said.

And when I had asked him if it were an actress who had to follow everything carefully, he replied :

" You! "

And for some reason I got more and more convinced that this " you " was I. The whole of that day I spent in a state of turmoil.

The theatre was full. There were many people I knew there. My seat was in the dress circle, on the right, near the door, and at such a height that I could shake hands with the friends who came in and hear everything the people who stood at the door or came through it were saying. It seemed to me that everybody was as excited and expectant as I was.

The first act began.

It is very difficult to describe the feeling with which I looked and listened. The play seemed to have no meaning for me. It seemed to get entirely lost. I strained my ears to catch every word of every character who might be speaking. I listened with the greatest possible attention. But I could not make anything out of the play and it left no impression on me. When Nina Zarechnaya began her monologue, " People, lions, eagles . . ." I heard a curious noise in the stalls and I seemed to come to with a start. What was the matter? It seemed to me that suppressed laughter passed over the rows of people below ; or wasn't it laughter, but an indignant murmur? Whatever it was, it was something unpleasant, something hostile. But it couldn't be! Chekhov was so popular! He was such a favourite with everybody!

The curtain came down, and suddenly something indescribable happened : the applause was drowned by boos, and the more people applauded, the louder was the booing. And it was then that I could clearly hear the people laugh. And they did not just laugh : they roared with laughter. The audience began to come out into the corridors and the foyer, and I heard how some of them were highly indignant, while others gave vent to their disapproval in bitter and venomous words.

" Some symbolic trash! " " Why doesn't he stick to his short stories ? " " Who does he take us for ? " " Giving himself airs! Getting careless! "

The writer Yassinsky came up to me. He was out of breath and dishevelled.

" How did you like it ? Why, it's frightful! It's shameful, disgusting! "

Someone took him away. Many people passed with a malicious grin on their faces, others waved their arms about or shook their heads. From everywhere I could hear: Chekhov . . . Chekhov . . . Chekhov. . . .

Even if I had wanted to, I should not have been able to get up. But I did not want to. Everything became quiet in the auditorium. They all went out, filled with venomous spite and eager to give full vent to their spleen. They gathered in small crowds, vying with each other in their loud condemnation of the play. The literary and journalistic fraternity! The same people who scraped and bowed before him, who flattered him so obsequiously. Why shouldn't they now be glad of the opportunity of kicking him hard so that it hurt. He had risen too fast and too high for their liking, and now they were eager to pull him down, imagining already that his proud head would never again rise above them.

After the interval, just as the auditorium began to fill, I

noticed Suvorin in one of the boxes to the left of me. I expected to see Chekhov too, but he was not there.

And once more I started following attentively every word of the play, though now I hardly hoped for any message from the stage. I remembered that Chekhov had written the play in summer in his little hut in Melikhovo. The little hut was surrounded by trees. From the house he would hear occasionally the sounds of the piano and singing. He felt happy when he was writing. He told me so himself. All this flashed through my mind so vividly that for a moment I could see the little hut and Chekhov sitting over his manuscript with a strand of hair falling over his forehead. Petersburg with the Alexandrinsky Theatre was far away then, the first night was far away, but now it was Melikhovo, his quiet and happy retreat, that was far away, and instead of his little hut there was the packed auditorium of a theatre and the faces of his friends which had suddenly been transformed into the faces of ferocious beasts.

The play was a dismal failure. What was Chekhov feeling now? Who was there with him to make him feel the presence of a friend at his side? Who was there to comfort him? How I'd have envied that person if I had known him!

As for his reply from the stage, he must have been joking after all. He had said it to someone he didn't know—just in case.

But presently—Nina came out to say goodbye to Trigorin. She handed him a medallion and said: "I have had your initials engraved on one side, and the title of your book on the other."

"What a lovely present!" said Trigorin, kissing the medallion.

Nina went out—and Trigorin, examining his present, turned it over and read: "Page 121, lines 11 and 12." Twice he repeated the numbers and asked Arkadina, who had just come in, " Have you any of my books in the house ? "

And already with the book in his hands, he repeated : " Page 121, lines 11 and 12." And when he found the page and counted the lines, he read softly but clearly : " If you ever want my life, come and take it."

From the very beginning, as soon as Nina stretched out her hand with the medallion, something queer happened to me : at first I went numb and I could hardly breathe, then I lowered my head because it seemed to me that everyone in the theatre, as one man, had turned round and was peering into my face. My head was in a whirl, my heart pounded like mad. But I did not miss or forget anything : page 121, lines 11 and 12. The numbers were different. They were not the same I had engraved on my present to Chekhov, the watch-chain pendant I had sent him. That certainly was his answer. He had given me his reply from the stage, after all, me, only me, and not Yavorskaya or anyone else.

" To you! You! " He knew he was talking to me. He was with me the whole time, and he knew that he was with me. That meant that he must have recognised me at once. At the first glance. But what was in those lines ? What was in those lines ?

I was again in a position to look at the stage, and now I could follow the play. But most of all I wanted to see Chekhov. He was not in the box and that meant that he was behind the scenes. It was quite impossible to go there. And even if it were possible, I shouldn't have had the courage to go. If only I could have met him by accident so that I could find out whether he wanted me to be near him or not. Would he have resented my presence ? Oh, if only I knew whether he wanted to see me! But I could not help feeling that just then, at that terrible moment of his life, he would scarcely have recognised me. He would probably have gone past me and even been annoyed to have run across me. He had given me his reply from the stage in a play that was a failure and that would have made him resent my presence all the more. It was not for nothing that I was afraid of him, as though I were guilty. But during the last interval I could not restrain myself and rushed through all the corridors and the foyer. I should have been able to tell at once by the look on his face whether he needed me or not.

But I could not find him anywhere, and later I heard people saying that Chekhov had run away from the theatre. Everybody was whispering about it as they retailed this piece of news to each other. He had run away!

In the last act, which I liked very much and which for a time even made me forget the failure of the play, Kommissarzhevskaya (Nina), recalling Treplyov's play in which she had acted the World Soul in the first act, suddenly tore off a sheet from the sofa, wrapped it round herself, and again began her monologue, " People, lions, eagles. . . ."

But she had barely time to start when the whole theatre began to roar with laughter. And that in the most dramatic and most moving place in the play which should have made everyone cry!

They laughed at the sheet, and as a matter of fact Kommissarzhevskaya, in her eagerness to remind the audience of the white peplum of the World Soul, was not quite successful in representing it beautifully enough, but that was all the same merely an excuse and not the real reason for the laughter. I was convinced that it was those animal faces that began laughing intentionally and that the audience became infected or perhaps even imagined that one was expected to laugh at that place. Be that as it may, everyone roared with laughter, the entire theatre laughed, and the end of the play was completely ruined. No one was moved by the shot that put an end to Treplyov's life and the curtain came down to the accompaniment of the same boos and jeers which had drowned the few timid claps at the end of the first act.

In the cloakroom the excitement had not died down yet. There, too, they were laughing. They were abusing the author loudly, shouting at each other:

" Did you hear? He ran away! I'm told he went straight to the railway station. Gone back to Moscow! "

" In his tails? All dressed up to take his bow! Ha-ha! "

But I also overheard one woman say to her companion:

" What a pity! Such a sympathetic man! Such a talent! And so young! He's still a very young man, isn't he? "

At home a cold supper and a boiling *samovar* were waiting for me. Michael, too, was there.

" Well? A great success? "

" A failure," I replied unwillingly. " A terrible failure."

" Don't go to the nursery," he warned me, taking hold of my hand. " I was there a minute ago. They're all peacefully asleep. They had a lovely time, ran about, played games. Sit down and tell me all about the play."

" It was a failure," I repeated, and I told him roughly all that I had seen and heard.

" Oh, what scoundrels those newspaper scribblers are! " Michael said warmly. " Toadies, swine. . . . You say Chekhov ran away? Well, you can imagine what he must feel. I'm afraid plays are not in his line. He should write things like *The Steppe*. That's where he is inimitable! "

What a relief to hear Michael abusing his enemies and detractors and not Chekhov! I had expected him to take advantage of this occasion to make some unfriendly remarks about him, but it seemed he felt sorry for Chekhov and forgot his hostility to him.

"Don't worry, mother," he said. "That's nothing. Let them boo him. He'll soon show them the kind of stuff he's made of. They'll be running after him with their tails between their legs as before, but next time they need not expect him to be so kind to them. Your Chekhov is too good-natured: ready to fall on the neck of every dirty rascal he comes across."

I listened to him and felt pleased, but I could not get those numbers out of my head: 121, 11 and 12.

Chekhov's book was on a shelf in Michael's study. It was not difficult to find. Find and read his message to me. But I had to have my tea first, eat my ham sandwiches, listen to Michael and talk to him. But what did I expect to find there? On page 121, lines 11 and 12? Oh, if only I could get hold of his book now, at once!

At length I finished my tea. Michael went to his study, pottered about there, whistled some tune, and at last went through the drawing-room to the bedroom.

"Will you be coming soon, mother?"

"Yes, presently."

It was only then that I, too, went into the study. I had to light a candle, for Michael had put out the lamp, and, candle in hand, I quickly found Chekhov's book, took it out, and with trembling fingers found page 121. Having counted the lines, I read: " . . .est phenomena. But why do you look at me like that? Do you like me?"

Dumbfounded, I reread the lines. No, I had made no mistake: " . . .est phenomena . . ."

"Mother! Old girl!" shouted Michael. "What are you doing there?"

" Why do you look at me like that ? . . ." I closed the book slowly and put it back on the shelf. Had he been making fun of me after all ?

" Do you like me ? "

He was in the train now on the way to Moscow. Sitting down and thinking. No, he would hardly be thinking of anything now. He must be trying to forget what he could not help seeing and hearing in his mind : the bewildered actors on the stage, the faces of those beasts in the auditorium, booing, laughter. Oh, I knew his state of mind very well. I had been through it myself. But does he also remember his " reply " ? Does he realise what I, who had been waiting for it with such breathless impatience, would feel like when I read, " Do you like me ? " Was it worth his while putting in the episode with the medallion for that ?

I could not sleep. I, too, was pursued by the memories of what I had seen in the theatre, by the impressions of that frightful failure and by my own disappointment. " Do you like me ? "

And suddenly the thought flashed through my mind : I had chosen the lines in his book, but mightn't he have chosen the lines in mine ?

Michael had long been asleep. I jumped out of bed and ran to the study. I found my little volume *The Happy Man*, and there on page 121, lines 11 and 12, I read : " It is not proper for young ladies to go to mask balls."

So that was his reply! A reply to many things : to the question who had sent him the watch pendant and who was the woman in the mask. He had guessed everything. He knew everything.

NINE

SOME TRANSLATED play was being performed at Suvorin's theatre. Looking round the auditorium, I suddenly saw Chekhov sitting next to Suvorin in the latter's box. I did not know he was in Petersburg. Why had he not written to tell me that he was coming? What a strange friendship ours was! He saw me and turned away. And how funny it was! How absurd! Mr. and Mrs. Suvorin and Chekhov sandwiched between them! And Chekhov knew I " adored " him and that was probably why he had turned his back on me. Was he wearing my watch-chain pendant, I wondered.

In the interval I went into the foyer. As I was hurrying down the stairs after the bell, I saw Chekhov. He was standing in the corridor at the door of his box, the same box where we had once been drinking champagne. Seeing me, he quickly came up and took my hand.

" It's a stupid play," he said hurriedly. " Don't you agree ? It's not worth seeing it to the end. May I see you home ? You're alone, aren't you ? "

" Pray, don't trouble yourself," I replied. " If you go away, you'll displease Suvorin."

Chekhov frowned.

" You're angry. But where and how can I speak to you ? It's important."

" And do you think that the best place to speak to me is in the street ? "

" But please tell me : where ? when ? "

The door of the box opened and Suvorin appeared.

" You see, they're looking for you. Go back to your seat quickly! " I laughed and walked off rapidly along the corridor.

" Well, it's clear enough," I said to myself maliciously, " that I've got over my attack."

I wanted to go back to my seat, but I changed my mind, went to the cloakroom, got out my coat and went home. As a matter of fact, it was snowing and raining at the same time. Strong gusts of wind made it hard to walk.

" Cab, ma'am ? " said a cabman.

I hesitated for a moment, and then walked on. I did not want to go home, and, besides, it was too early : I was not expected back so soon.

" What a clever way of talking and acting," I reproached myself bitterly. " Got over your attack! Oh dear, how wretched I am! And he wanted to have a talk with me. What about ? ' It's important,' he said. And I have offended him again! "

I thought it over and then decided sadly, " No! He understood me. He understands everything. He knows everything. Now he is looking at my empty seat and feeling sad."

But why sad? Because he is sorry for me?
Oh, if only he too had been in love with me! If . . .
And then what?
I walked and walked for hours, for I could find no answer
my last question.

TEN

WE ARRANGED to meet in Moscow. I had to be there in March, and Chekhov promised to come from Melikhovo.

On 18th March 1897 he wrote to me:

"Angry Lydia Alexeyevna, I should very much like to see you—very much, in spite of the fact that you are angry with me and wish me all the best 'in any case'. I shall be in Moscow before the 26th of March, probably on Monday, at ten o'clock in the evening, and I shall be staying at the Moscow Grand Hotel, opposite Iverskaya Street. I may possibly come earlier if my work permits. I am, alas, very busy at the moment. I hope to remain in Moscow till the 28th, and then, believe it or not, I shall be leaving for Petersburg. Good-bye till then. Turn your anger to mercy and agree to have lunch or dinner with me. I promise you everything will be all right. I press your hand. With my humblest regards,

"Your Chekhov."

I sent him my Moscow address, and on 23rd March I received a note from him by messenger :

" Moscow Grand Hotel. Room 5. Saturday.

" I arrived in Moscow earlier than I expected. When shall we meet ? The weather is misty and foul, and I'm feeling a little indisposed. I shall try to stay indoors. Won't you come and see me without waiting for me to pay you a visit ? I wish you all the best. Your Chekhov."

I sent word to him at once that I should be at his hotel in the evening.

I was staying in Moscow with my elder brother who was married to my husband's sister. That was why I did not tell them at home that I was going to see Chekhov. My brother Alexey knew all about it and he arranged everything so that I did not have to make any excuses to explain my absence in the evening. He took advantage of the fact that it was my name-day and he invited me to his place. My elder brother and his wife were Tolstoyans, and they did not recognise name-days and avoided all name-day celebrations. However, that was true only of my brother and not of his wife. She would have been glad to spend the evening at Alexey's, to meet his friends, to have dinner and even a drink. But Alexey said to her, " I'm not inviting you : my rooms are very small and you're so large! " She was hurt and said that she would not have gone even if he had asked her.

I promised Alexey to go to his place later, for I did not expect to spend much time at the hotel.

As I had promised in my letter, I arrived at the hotel at eight o'clock.

The porter took my coat and I began to mount the stairs to Room 5.

Suddenly the porter called after me :

" Who do you want to see, ma'am ? "

" Mr. Chekhov. Room 5."

" I'm afraid he's not in. He's gone out."

" Impossible! He probably left instructions not to admit any visitors. He's ill. He wrote to me."

" I don't know anything about that, ma'am. Only he isn't in. He left with Mr. Suvorin in the morning."

I stood on the stairs completely at a loss.

A waiter came running in.

" The lady doesn't believe me that Mr. Chekhov isn't in," said the porter to him.

" I think he went back to his country place, ma'am," said the waiter. " I heard him say so to Mr. Suvorin. ' I shall be returning home in the evening,' he said. They had gone out to have lunch at the Slav Bazaar. He most probably decided not to come back."

" But he asked me to come. I wrote to him."

" There are hundreds of letters and notes for him here," said the porter. " Been arriving since morning."

I came down quickly. There was a heap of letters on the mirror. I went through it hastily, found my letter and crumpled it in my hand. Now I was sure that Chekhov was not at the hotel. I put on my coat and went away. While I was putting on my coat, the waiter went on propounding his theories.

" Mr. Chekhov's certain to have gone back to the country, ma'am. Some extra special business or something. . . ."

I took a cab and went to Alexey's.

I found lots of people there already, and it was getting noisy and gay.

" I changed my mind," I said to Alexey in reply to his puzzled look.

When they started playing the piano and singing I felt so miserable that I could not stand it any longer and hid myself in Alexey's little bedroom.

Soon Alexey joined me there. He looked very worried, but apparently he did not have the heart to pester me with questions and just gazed at me silently. The room was lit only by a little icon lamp.

When I told him of my reception at the hotel, he jumped to his feet.

" What do you suppose has happened ? " he asked.

" I expect Suvorin must have dragged him off somewhere and he forgot all about me."

" And I tell you it's impossible! Chekhov ? Never! Either those scoundrels at the hotel have made some mistake or—I don't know what! At any rate, it's impossible to leave it like that. We must find out what's happened."

" But how ? "

" Let's go there at once. I'll go in and find out. Quite possibly he's back by now."

" But I—I don't want to see him. Nothing in the world would induce me to see him now! "

" If you like I'll speak to him. What shall I say ? "

" Don't know. I don't know anything. Not now. You'd better not go to him at all. Better not speak to him. Just find out. . . ."

" But I'm sure Chekhov couldn't have acted like that. It can't be Suvorin. Something important must have happened. Come on, let's go! "

" And your guests ? "

" They'll be all right without me. Nanny will look after them."

We did not take a cab, but walked to the hotel, though it

was a long way from my brother's place. It was such a lovely spring day, and the air was so balmy! It had rained a short while ago and even the cobbles in the road exuded a fragrance. There was not a trace of snow anywhere. Spring was early that year. I was told that the river was no longer ice-bound.

We walked and talked about Chekhov.

Alexey went into the hotel alone, but spent no more than a few minutes there. He took my arm and we walked back.

" He hasn't returned," he said. " They told me he was ill when he arrived. I'll make further inquiries tomorrow."

It was starting to rain again and soon it was raining cats and dogs. The air got even warmer and more fragrant.

Next day Alexey came to see me and told me that Chekhov was seriously ill. He had been taken to a private clinic.

On the morning of the 25th I received this note from him :

" Moscow, March 1897.

" Here's my *curriculum vitae* : on Saturday night I started coughing up blood. In the morning I left for Moscow. At six o'clock I went with Suvorin to the Hermitage Restaurant to have dinner, but no sooner had I sat down at table than blood started pouring out of my throat in good earnest. Then Suvorin took me to the Slav Bazaar. Doctors were called in. I lay there for more than a day and now I am at home, that is, in the Moscow Hotel. Your A. Chekhov.

" Monday."

About three o'clock in the afternoon on Tuesday Alexey and I went to the clinic. In the waiting-room we were met by a woman in a white uniform : a Sister or the Matron, I don't know which.

" This is my sister," said Alexey. " She'd like to see Mr. Chekhov."

The woman in the white uniform looked horrified. She raised her arms and shoulders.

"Impossible! Quite impossible! Mr. Chekhov is very weak. Miss Chekhov alone is permitted to see him."

"But can't we have a few words with the doctor?"

"The doctor? But he won't be able to do anything for you. He'll only tell you the same thing."

"Still I'd like to see the doctor if I may."

Sister shrugged, thought it over, and went out.

The doctor came and said at once, "It's impossible to see Mr. Chekhov. I'm afraid I can't permit you to see him."

Here I spoke up.

"In that case will you please tell him that I received his note today and—and that I came but was not allowed to see him."

"You received a note from him today? But he fell ill the day before yesterday."

I produced Chekhov's letter and gave it to him.

"He wrote it yesterday."

The doctor pushed the letter away and knit his brows.

"Wait, please," he said and left the room quickly.

"See? He'll let you see him," said Alexey.

When the doctor came back, he first gave me a long look, shook his head, and spread out his hands in a gesture of helpless submission.

"I don't know what to do," he said. "Mr. Chekhov insists that he must see you. Wait. . . . You're on a visit to Moscow, aren't you?"

"Yes."

"And it was to see you that he came to Moscow in this weather although he was feeling ill?"

"Suvorin arrived . . ." I began.

The doctor gave a knowing smile.

" Yes, yes! And to see Suvorin he risked his life ? You see, madam, he's dangerously ill and the slightest excitement may have serious consequences. Of course you know best what you're doing. I can't be responsible for anything. I'm sorry, but that's the position."

I was dismayed.

" What shall I do ? Go away ? "

" You can't go away now. He's expecting you. He's very excited. I'm afraid there's nothing we can do now. We'd better go."

We began ascending the stairs.

" For God's sake don't talk to him. Not a word, whatever he says. It's dangerous. Remember, if you talk to him he may have another haemorrhage. I give you three minutes. Three minutes, no more. Here. . . . Well," he added in a gentler tone, " don't look so worried. It'll be all right. I'll come in in three minutes."

Chekhov was alone in the room. He lay on his back, his head turned to the door.

" How kind you are . . ." he said softly.

" You mustn't talk," I interrupted him, frightened. " How do you feel ? Have you any pain ? "

He smiled and motioned me to the chair beside his bed.

" Three minutes," I said, and took his watch from the table.

He took his watch away and kept my hand in his.

" Tell me, would you have come ? "

" To you ? But, my dear, I did come."

" You did ? "

" Please don't talk. You mustn't. And, besides, it's not important."

" What ? "

" That I came and . . ."

" Not important ? Not important ? "

" The only important thing now is that you should get well as soon as possible."

He frowned.

" So it isn't important ? "

" All right, we'll discuss it another time, shall we ? "

He smiled.

" I'm very weak," he whispered.

" What shall I tell you to keep you quiet ? "

" Are you going back today ? "

" No, tomorrow."

" You'll come to see me tomorrow, won't you ? You must come. I'll be waiting. You'll come ? "

" Of course I will."

The doctor came in and turned to Chekhov with a pleasant smile. " I'm afraid it's time, Anton Pavlovich," he said. " You mustn't tire yourself."

" One more minute. Lydia Alexeyevna, I'd like to ask you something. . . ."

The doctor raised an admonitory finger and then handed him a small sheet of paper and a pencil. Chekhov wrote :

" Take my proofs from Goltsev at *Russian Thought* and bring me something of your own to read and something else."

When I had read his note, he took it from me and added :

" I lo . . . thank you very much."

He crossed out " lo . . ." and smiled.

I said good-bye and went to the door. Suddenly Chekhov called me back.

" Lydia Alexeyevna," he said, " you look like a famous actress on tour."

" It's my dress," I said, laughing. " The Seagull."

The doctor grew indignant.

" Anton Pavlovich! You're a doctor yourself. If you're not better by tomorrow, I shan't let anyone visit you. No one! "

Alexey and I walked home and all the time I was wiping away the tears which rolled down my face.

Alexey was breathing hard and sighing.

" Don't be sorry for me, Alexey," I said. " I feel grand . . . grand! "

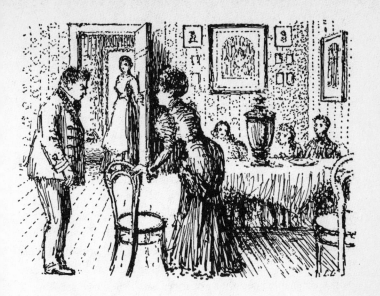

ELEVEN

AT HOME I found two telegrams. One : " Hope to meet you 27 stop miss you very much." The other : " Come immediately stop waiting stop kisses."

Next morning another telegram : " Wire when leaving stop expecting you tomorrow for certain."

I went to the office of *Russian Thought* to see Goltsev and get Chekhov's proofs.

Goltsev was surprised.

" What does he want his proofs for now ? There's plenty of time."

On learning that I had been at the clinic, he began to ply me with questions about Chekhov's condition and called in a few more people.

" Here. . . . Latest news about Chekhov."

" It's bad it's spring now," someone said. " The ice on the

river began breaking up yesterday. It's the most dangerous season for that kind of illness."

" I've heard that his condition is very bad," said someone else. " He's on the danger list. . . ."

" So he's allowed to receive visitors ? "

"No, no," said Goltsev. "Mrs. Avilova will give him our best regards and good wishes for a speedy recovery. And please tell him there's no hurry about the proofs. Don't let him tire himself."

I left the office of *Russian Thought* feeling very worried. The impression Chekhov had made on me was that of a dying man and there they said that he was very bad and mentioned the river. . . . " The most dangerous season. . . ." I couldn't help feeling that they thought there was little hope for him.

It was too early for the clinic (they would not have admitted me before two o'clock) and I went to the river.

On Zamoskvorechye Bridge I went up to the railings and began looking down on the river. The icefloes were no longer large. Sometimes they covered the whole stretch of the river and sometimes the river was completely free of ice. It was a sunny day, a strangely blue and radiant day, but to me it seemed to harbour some menace, a menace that seemed also to be hidden in the turbulent and impatient river that flowed swiftly under the bridge. Icefloes appeared, circled round and round, and disappeared in the distance. It seemed to me that the river flowed swifter and ever swifter, and that made me feel a little dizzy.

There. . . . The river bit into an icefloe, gnawed at it, broke it up, and was carrying it away. And life, too, rushed along like a river, gnawing at everything, breaking it up, and sweeping it away. " The most dangerous season. . . ." " Chekhov's bad! Very bad! "

I remembered the seal with which he had recently begun to seal his letters. On the small red circle of the sealing-wax the words were clearly imprinted : " To the lonely the world's a desert."

" Till my thirtieth birthday I hadn't a worry in the world," he had told me once.

And had life got the better of him after his thirtieth birthday and begun to break him up ?

Life! Could it ever have satisfied such an exceptional being as Chekhov ? Could it have prevented his soul from being poisoned by wrongs and bitterness ? His great, pure soul which put such high demands on itself ?

No sooner had the fever of youth left him, no sooner had he passed the time of life when his breast was full of the joy of living, no sooner had he cast his eyes round him seriously and unsparingly than he began to feel himself in a desert, lonely. At first, perhaps, this feeling was vague, but it grew more and more definite, more and more palpable. Why else should he have got himself such a seal ? Quite possibly he did not realise himself, perhaps he did not even know that he was head and shoulders above everyone else, and that for a man of his stature there could be no happiness in life. Not yet, at any rate.

Then for some reason I remembered something very funny.

" Why did you send me twenty copecks ? " Chekhov had asked me.

" Twenty copecks ? "

" Why, yes. You gave it to the railway porter at Lopasnya Station* and told him to give it to me."

" I gave him a note for you! "

" The porter had dirtied the note so much that I couldn't make anything out, except perhaps your signature. But the

* The station of Chekhov's Melikhovo estate.

twenty-copeck piece was as clean as a whistle. I took it."

This " I took it " made me laugh every time I remembered it.

And the river flowed swiftly on and on. . . .

No! Chekhov will not die! . . . It is madness to think of it, it's . . .

And I nearly dropped the packet which I held under my arm. I tossed my head and quickly went down to the bank of the river.

I went to buy flowers. Chekhov had written : " And something else. . . ." Well, let the flowers be that " something else ".

I arrived at the clinic just in time. Sister met me.

" No, Mr. Chekhov is no better," she replied to my question. " He hardly slept during the night. He's spitting more blood now."

" So I shan't be able to see him ? "

" I asked the doctor and he told me to let you see him."

Sister was evidently displeased and she kept looking disapprovingly at me.

I tore off the thin paper from the flowers.

" Good gracious," exclaimed Sister, " you can't do that! Don't you realise that the smell of the flowers in the room of a t.b. patient . . ."

I was frightened.

" In that case you'd better take them. Take them."

She smiled.

" Well, I suppose you could take them to him now that you've brought them. We'll take them out of his room later."

In his room I was at once met by the same tender, appealing look.

He took the flowers in both hands and buried his face in them.

"My favourite ones," he whispered. "Roses and lilies of the valley. How beautiful they are!"

Sister said:

"But I'm afraid you can't have them in your room. The doctor won't allow it."

"I'm a doctor myself," said Chekhov. "You can leave them. Put them in water, please."

Sister threw me another unfriendly glance and went out.

"You're late," said Chekhov, pressing my hand weakly.

"No, I'm not. I was told not to come before two and it's two now."

"It's seven minutes past two, my dear child. Seven minutes! And I was waiting, waiting. . . ."

He began to look through the newspapers and books which I had brought. He put the proofs on the table and listened to the account of my visit to Goltsev.

"I'm afraid I've read them all," he was saying softly. "Unpublished articles of Tolstoy? The last ones? Yes, I'll read that with pleasure. I don't share . . ."

"You mustn't talk," I interrupted him, "and you seem about to embark on an analysis of Tolstoy's teachings."

"When are you going back?"

"Today."

"No, don't. Stay another day. Come and see me tomorrow. Please, I ask you. I ask you!"

I took out the three telegrams and showed them to him. He studied them a long time.

"I think you could stay one more day."

"I'm worried by this 'come immediately'. I hope the children are all right."

" I'm certain everyone's all right. Stay one more day for my sake. For my sake," he repeated.

I said softly, " I'm awfully sorry, but I can't."

I just imagined what would happen if I did stay. I'd have to send a telegram to say that I had been detained, and Michael would immediately leave for Moscow. Well, suppose he didn't ; suppose he waited for my arrival. What kind of a reception could I expect from him ? And that wouldn't have mattered! But I knew that if we had a scene I should have had to tell him that I was in love with Chekhov and that I should have acted in such a way that nothing would have been left of our happy married life. His life and mine would have been turned into a hell on earth. And because of what ? Because of another visit to the clinic lasting three minutes. . . .

Thoughts raced wildly through my head.

" So it's impossible," said Chekhov.

And once again I could see that he knew everything and understood everything. Michael's jealousy and my fear. What did he say ? " I'm sure they're all right."

The doctor came in. Chekhov pointed at the flowers and said firmly :

" It can't do me any harm."

The doctor bent down, smelt the flowers, and said vaguely, " Oh, very well."

Then he turned to me.

" Our patient is behaving very badly : doesn't sleep, is excited." He laughed and added, " Headstrong. Difficult to manage."

I realised that the doctor did not approve of my visits and that he would be glad if I left Moscow.

" Are you leaving today ? " he asked, as though guessing my thoughts.

" Tonight."

" If it's only tonight . . ." Chekhov began quickly, but glancing at the doctor, did not finish the sentence.

" You must have a good rest, a good rest," the doctor kept repeating.

It was time to say good-bye and go, but I was so absorbed in my thoughts that I hardly realised what I was doing. I started collecting the papers and books on his bed and wrapping them up. But turning round accidentally I saw that Chekhov was smiling slyly and shielding the flowers with both hands. I recollected myself, laughed, and replaced the parcel on the bed.

" Get well! " I said, pressing Chekhov's hand which lay lifelessly on the blanket.

" Pleasant journey," he said.

I went quickly to the door, but, as before, he called me back.

" I shall be in Petersburg at the end of April. At the beginning of May at the latest."

" Of course, of course! " said the doctor.

" But I must! " Chekhov cried excitedly.

" Of course, of course! "

" I'm speaking seriously! So that at the end of April . . . I'll be there for certain."

" Meanwhile we shall write to each other," I said, and, catching the doctor's stern look, left the room quickly.

This time I did not feel grand. I had refused Chekhov's warm request : " . . . for my sake." And for his sake I could not do such a little thing as stay another day in Moscow.

" I ask you . . ."

I was walking home feeling very depressed, accusing and justifying myself, when suddenly I saw Tolstoy standing before me. He often went for a walk in Devichy Square. He recognised me and stopped.

" Where are you coming from ? A monastery ? "

" No, from the clinic."

I told him about Chekhov.

" Yes, I knew that he'd fallen ill, but I did not think they'd let anyone visit him. I'll go and see him tomorrow."

" Yes, please do, Leo Nikolayevich. I'm sure he'll be very glad. I know he's very fond of you."

" I'm very fond of him, too," replied Tolstoy. " The only thing I can't understand is why he's writing plays."

" Here," I thought to myself, " is a man who would have condemned me mercilessly if he knew what was going on inside me now."

I wanted desperately to see someone who would not be unsympathetic or indifferent to what I was so agonisingly experiencing just then, and I went to see Alexey.

TWELVE

IN THE railway carriage that night I could not sleep. I could not cope with my confused and complicated thoughts and feelings. I lay worrying all night. Dawn was just beginning to break when I suddenly found myself on the seashore. The sea was leaden and sullen beneath a low-lying leaden and sullen sky. One wave followed another, all with white-flecked crests, and broke with an incessant roar at my feet. Chekhov was walking beside me. He was saying something, but his words were lost in the roar of the waves. Suddenly I caught a glimpse of something small and white moving in the distance. It was getting nearer and nearer. It was a little boy. He was running to meet us, skipping and shouting happily. He could not be more than two or three years old.

"Look, a little boy!" I cried. "How did a little boy get here? And such a happy, lovely child, too!"

Chekhov gave a start and stopped.

"It isn't a child," he said in a strangled voice. "No, no! It isn't a child! I know! He's pretending!"

"Who?" I asked, feeling that my feet suddenly refused to move from horror.

"What sort of a child is this?" Chekhov went on, stopping before me as though wishing to protect me and hide me from the child. "Look! There's blood on his mouth! His mouth is covered with blood!"

The child was near us now, and he was still running along, waving his little hands and shouting happily.

"We must throw him into the sea!" shouted Chekhov. "Into the sea! Into the sea! But I can't. I can't. I ca-a-an't!"

I woke up shaking with terror. The train was thundering over a bridge. The engine was emitting a long drawn-out, shrill whistle.

The dawn was still breaking. How long could I have been asleep? A minute perhaps. No more.

Michael saw me while I was still standing at the window. He came in with a porter, showed him my things, took my arm and helped me out of the carriage. All I asked was:

"How are the children?"

"They're all right. Everything's all right."

We went out of the station.

While embracing the children in the drawing-room, I heard an explosion of Michael's temper: this time it was our maid's fault because there was a smell of something that shouldn't have been there.

"Welcome home, darling! Had a good journey?"

" My journey was all right, but my homecoming is not so pleasant."

" Oh, very well, very well! " said Michael with a wave of the hand. " Never mind that. Come, old girl, let's have coffee. Bring your mother, children. The coffee's steaming hot! "

And again my life slipped into its usual groove. Again the same old domestic worries, again the same constant alarms about the children's health, again Michael's customary fastidiousness and irritability, quarrels, reconciliations, occasional disgraceful scenes, visitors, theatres.

On the 29th I received a letter from Chekhov.

" Moscow, 28th March 1897.

" Your flowers do not fade but are getting lovelier. My colleagues have given me permission to have them on the table. You are, on the whole, good, very good, and I don't know how to thank you. They will not let me out of here before Easter, which means that I shan't be in Petersburg soon. I am feeling much better ; there is less blood. But I am still bedridden and I am writing my letters lying down. I hope you are well. I press your hand firmly. Your Chekhov."

My flowers . . .

Moscow seemed unreal to me already. Like a dream. And it also seemed to me that I had invented both the stairs to Chekhov's room and his tiny room with the bed, table, and chair, and his dear, dear face on the pillow, and his dark, tender, appealing eyes.

And now he was lying there, and my flowers were beside him on the table, but he was no longer expecting me. I had refused to stay another day " for his sake ", even one more day. Now he understood me perfectly and he was smiling sadly to himself. " To the lonely the world's a desert."

" Pleasant journey," he had said.

Oh, how different everything seemed to me now from what it had been in Moscow! And how suddenly I found myself miles and miles away from Chekhov! And how gradually and imperceptibly I came to despise myself sincerely! Even to write to Chekhov seemed impossible to me now.

I cannot get out of my mind one of Chekhov's stories. I believe it is called *A Little Joke*.

A winter evening. Wind. An ice-covered hill. A young man and a young girl are tobogganing. And every time the toboggan glides swiftly down the hill and the wind whistles in their ears, the young girl hears the words, " I love you, Nadya ".

But perhaps she is only imagining it.

They climb up to the top of the hill again. Again they sit down on the sledge. Now it precipitates itself over the top, they rush down. . . . And again she hears the same words, " I love you, Nadya ".

Who said it ? The wind ? Or the one who was sitting behind her ?

The moment they come to a stop everything is just as usual, and the face of her companion looks indifferent.

It was I who had been rushing down the hill in Moscow. Before, too, I had been rushing down a hill. Not for the first time had I heard the words, " I love you ", but after a short time everything became usual and ordinary, and Chekhov's letters were cold and indifferent.

Chekhov did not come to Petersburg in the spring, and in the autumn the doctors sent him to Nice. He wrote to me from there : " I shall probably spend the whole winter abroad." He also wrote : " I feel tolerably well in the morning and exceedingly well in the evening."

He wrote that in October. And at the beginning of November : " Everything was all right while the weather was cold, but now when it is raining and beastly, I have again a rasping feeling in my throat, and again there is blood. What a damn nuisance! "

I sent him my published stories, and he sent me back detailed criticisms.

" Oh, Lydia Alexeyevna, I read your *Forgotten Letters* with such great delight! It is a good, clever, exquisite thing. It is a dock-tailed little thing, but there is so much art and talent in it that I can't understand why you do not carry on in the same style. Letters are a silly, boring form of writing, and, besides, so easy, but what I have in mind is the tone, the sincere, almost passionate feeling, and the graceful phrase. Goltsev was right when he said that you possessed an attractive talent, and if you still do not believe it, it is your own fault. You spend too little time on your work. You are lazy. I, too, am a lazy Ukrainian peasant, but compared with you I have written mountains of things. Apart from the *Forgotten Letters*, inexperience, lack of confidence, and laziness peep out from between the lines of every story. You are not, as they say, a practised hand yet, and you work like a beginner, like a young lady painting on porcelain. You feel a landscape and you describe it very well, but you don't know how to economise, and one comes across the same landscape over and over again where it is not wanted, and one of your stories even gets lost among the masses of descriptive passages which are heaped up in a pile throughout the whole story from the beginning to (almost) the middle of it. Then you do not work on a sentence. Every sentence has to be carefully wrought—that is where art comes in. You must eliminate everything that is superfluous, clean it of ' as much as ' and ' with the help of ', you must think of its rhythm. . . .

You must never use rough, clumsy words that are to be found only in colloquial speech, and you ought to feel their roughness, for you are musical and sensitive, which is proved by your *Forgotten Letters*. But don't take my criticism too much to heart, and send me something else of yours."

I am afraid I was a bad pupil and only understood Chekhov's advice later when I realised the necessity of " hearing " what I wrote and not using any word that occurred to me on the spur of the moment because it fitted the sense of what I wanted to express. There is no doubt in my mind, however, that this necessity arose only as a result of Chekhov's criticism. If I did not feel it at first, Chekhov's criticism gave me the push in the right direction, and if, in spite of everything, nothing came of it, it was only because I was a talented nonentity.

I was sure Chekhov realised it as well as I and that his attitude towards me was different from what it had been. When I wrote to him, I could not help feeling that I was forcing myself on him, but I could not stop our correspondence any more than I could have put an end to my life.

In the summer Chekhov returned to Russia, and at the end of April I received the following letter from him :

" There are so many visitors that I don't seem to have a free moment to reply to your last letter. I want to write you a long letter, but the thought that at any moment someone may come in and interfere with me keeps me away from my writing-desk. And, as a matter of fact, while putting down the word ' interfere ' a little girl came in and told me that a patient was waiting for me. I must go.

" The financial question has been satisfactorily solved. I have collected my little stories from *Fragments* and sold them to Sytin for ten years. Moreover, it seems I can now get a thousand roubles from *Russian Thought* where, incidentally, they just gave me a rise. They used to pay me two hundred and fifty, but now they are paying me three hundred.

" I am fed up with writing and I don't know what to do. I'd gladly take up medicine and get myself some job, but I'm afraid I have not enough physical resilience.

" When I am doing some writing now or thinking of writing something, I am overcome by a feeling of nausea as though I were eating cabbage soup from which a cockroach had just been removed—I apologise for the comparison. What disgusts me so much is not the writing itself as the literary *entourage* from which it is impossible to escape and which one seems to carry about with one everywhere as the earth carries about the atmosphere.

" The weather is lovely, but I'd like to go away somewhere. I have to send something to the August number of *Russian Thought* ; I have written it already, but I have still got to revise it. Keep well and happy. There is no room for the rat's tail, so for once let my signature be without a tail. Your Chekhov."

I was waiting very anxiously for the appearance of the August number of *Russian Thought*. I got used to reading between the lines of Chekhov's letters and now I had a feeling that he was drawing my attention very forcibly to the August number and that he wanted me to read it immediately. It is difficult to explain why I should have had that feeling, but it was so. I bought a copy of the journal as soon as it appeared instead of getting it out of the library as I usually did.

As soon as I read the title of Chekhov's story—*About Love* —I was thrown into violent agitation. I ran back home with the magazine in my hand and indulged in all sorts of conjectures. That *About Love* had something to do with me, I did not doubt for a moment. But what could he have written?

"Well, I expect I shall soon be reading an artistic appraisal of my personality," I thought. "And serves me right!"

I cut the journal in Michael's study and sat down at the desk to read it.

The love story of a man-cook and a parlourmaid. "She does not want to marry him but wants to live *so*," but he does not want to live *so* "because he is religious". It was not at all what I had expected.

But presently Luganovich invites Alyokhin to visit him and his wife, Anna Alexeyevna, appears. She has recently had a child. She is young and beautiful and makes a strong impression on Alyokhin. "Anna Alexeyevna Luganovich. . . ." I, too, had a baby when I first met Chekhov.

I remembered at once:

"But don't you think that when we first met we did not just become acquainted, but found each other after a long separation?"

That was what Chekhov had asked me at the anniversary dinner.

And I went on reading eagerly and impatiently.

" . . . I had no time even to think of the city, but the memory of the tall fair woman remained with me always; I did not think of her, but it was as though her light shadow lay on my soul."

A page later, after the second meeting, Alyokhin said:

"I was unhappy. At home, in the fields and in the barn I thought only of her. . . ."

Big tears began to drop on the paper, but I wiped them away hastily so that I could continue to read.

" For hours we spoke or kept silent, but we never avowed our love for one another. We concealed it timidly, jealously. We were afraid of everything that would reveal our secret to ourselves. I loved her deeply and tenderly, but I argued with myself, I asked myself what could be the outcome of our love if we had no strength to fight against it. It seemed incredible to me that my intense and sorrowful love should put a sudden end to the happy life of her husband, her children, her whole home. . . . Was it honest ? What would happen to her if I fell ill, if I died ?

" And apparently she thought the same. She thought of her husband, her children. . . ."

I was no longer crying, but sobbing hysterically. So he did not think I was to blame. He did not blame me, but justified me. He understood me. He grieved with me.

" . . . I felt that she was near me, that she was mine, that we could not live without one another. . . .

" During the last few years Anna Alexeyevna has been in a different mood. . . . She seems strangely irritable with me ; whatever I say, she contradicts. If I drop something, she will say coldly, ' You would! ' "

Oh yes, I remember how I used the identical words to him when one day he had dropped his hat in the mud. He probably wanted to brush back a strand of hair as usual, but instead his hand had gone over his hat.

Alyokhin and Anna said good-bye to one another for good in a railway carriage. She was going away.

" When there, in the compartment, our eyes met, we could no longer restrain ourselves. I embraced her, and she clung to me, her face buried on my chest, and tears gushed out of her eyes. . . . I realised that when you are in love your thoughts about this love must concern themselves with something that is higher and more important than happiness or unhappiness, virtue or vice, as these words are generally understood, or that it was much better not to think at all."

I finished reading the story and dropped my head on the book.

What that " higher " thing was I could not understand. And what was more important than happiness or unhappiness, virtue or vice, I did not know either. I knew and understood only one thing : that life had caught me as in a vice and that to free myself from the jaws of that vice was impossible. If my family prevented me from being happy with Chekhov, then Chekhov prevented me from being happy with my family. I had to tear myself in two.

What did he mean to convey by the words : " How unnecessary, trivial, and deceptive was everything that prevented us from loving one another ? "

I seized a sheet of paper and wrote a letter to Chekhov. I wrote without thinking what I was saying. But to make sure that I did not change my mind, I went out immediately and posted the letter. On my way back I was already sorry I had written it. It was not a kind letter.

In a few days I received a reply :

" 20th August. Melikhovo.

" I am about to leave for the Crimea, then for the Caucasus, and when it gets cold there I shall probably go somewhere abroad. Which means, I'm afraid, that I shall not be in Petersburg. I hate to have to go away. The thought that I have to leave makes me feel so unhappy and discouraged that I don't want to work. I can't help feeling that if I spent this winter in Moscow or Petersburg and lived in a nice, warm flat, I would recover from my illness entirely and would, moreover, work with such a will that, forgive the expression, the devil himself would be sick to look at me.

" This vagabond life, and during the winter months too—winter abroad is horrible—has thrown me off the rails completely.

" You are unfair to the bee. The first thing a bee sees is the beautiful bright flowers and it is only then that it takes the honey.

" As for the rest—indifference, boredom, and that men of talent live and love only in the world of their imagination—all I can say is : another man's soul is a dark well.

" The weather is beastly. Cold. Damp.

" I press your hand. Keep happy and well.

" Your Chekhov."

I remembered my letter.

I had thanked him for the honour of figuring as the heroine of one of his stories, very short though it was.

" I ran across one of your friends about whom his wife says that he is guilty of all sorts of mean and disgusting actions and that he does them so as to be able to give a realistic description of them in his novels. In the end, of course, he smites his breast in sorrow and remorse.

" You seem to exercise yourself in magnanimity and noble-mindedness. But, alas, you too are remorseful."

Then there were such sentences :

" How many themes must not a writer find before he is able to publish hundreds of long and short stories one after another. So that, like the bee, a writer has to take his honey where he can find it. . . . He is bored to tears with his writing, he is sick of it, but his hand has not lost its ' cunning ' and so he goes on coldly and indifferently describing feelings that his soul can no longer experience because his talent has driven his soul out of his body. And the colder the writer, the more sensitive and moving his story. Let the reader weep over it. That's what art is for, isn't it ? "

And in his reply there was not one, not one ill-tempered, spiteful line. He even expressed the desire to live in his hated Petersburg and complained of having to go away. If only he had uttered one word of reproach. If only he had made me feel ashamed of myself. Once only did he write to me : " Believe me, your severity does you no credit." That, I think, was the only time he ever rebuked me.

THIRTEEN

I HAD been greatly upset during the last months of 1898 : all my three children fell ill with whooping-cough, and at the same time my little Nina caught scarlet fever and before she had recovered Lyova went down with pneumonia.

In January 1899 everything was getting back to normal again, and at the very beginning of February I received a letter from Chekhov.

" 5th February, Yalta.

" Dear Lydia Alexeyevna,

" I have a great favour to ask you. A very boring request, I'm afraid. Please, don't be cross with me. Would you be so kind as to find someone, some well-behaved Miss, and commission her to copy out my stories published in *The Petersburg Gazette* some years ago. And also try to get the paper to give her permission to find and copy out my stories as it is very inconvenient to look them up and copy them in a public library. If for some reason you cannot carry out my request, then please forget about it, I shan't mind at all, but if it can be carried out in one way or another and if you can get someone to copy out my stories, then write to me and I will send you a list of the stories which have to be copied. I haven't the exact details and I have even forgotten the year in which my stories began to appear in *The Petersburg Gazette*. But when I hear from you that you have the copyist, I shall at once get in touch with an old bibliographer I know in Petersburg who will supply you with all the exact information. I implore you to forgive me if I am causing you any trouble and if I bore you with my request. I feel terribly ashamed, but after thinking it over carefully I have come to the conclusion that I have no one else to turn to. I want these stories badly. I must give them to Marx because of an agreement I have made with him and, worse luck, I have to read them again, edit them, and, as Pushkin says, ' reread my life with disgust '.

" How are you getting on ? Any news ?

" My health seems to be quite good ; during the winter I had another haemorrhage, but now there's no more blood and everything is all right.

" Write to me at least that you are not angry with me, if you don't feel like writing to me generally. We are having lovely weather in Yalta, but it is as dull as in Shklov. I am just like an army officer billeted in some godforsaken provincial hole. Well, I hope you are well, happy and successful in all your affairs. Remember me more often in your holy prayers, me the miserable sinner.   " Your Chekhov."

I find it hard to describe how happy this letter made me. To do some work for Chekhov—what joy it meant to me! And everything arranged itself beautifully : from the paper they sent me the bound half-yearly files of *The Petersburg Gazette*. Michael recommended two copyists. The only trouble was that no one seemed to remember the year in which Chekhov began contributing to the paper. I went for information to the old bibliographer Bykov. He was exceedingly nice, but he did not remember anything.

Of course I wrote to Chekhov immediately to tell him that I was starting operations, and received this reply from him :

" For your willingness to help me and for your dear, kind letter accept my very, very great thanks. I love letters which are not written in a sententious tone. You write that I seem to know how to make the best of life. Perhaps. But God sends the shrewd cow short horns. Of what use is the knowledge of making the best of life to me when I have to live away from everything as though I were in exile. I am like the man in the Russian saying who walked in Pea Street and found no peas ; I was free and never knew the meaning of freedom ; I was a literary man and was forced to spend all my life away from literary men ; I sold my works for seventy-five thousand roubles and have already received part of the money, but of what use is it to me when during the last fortnight I have been sitting at home all the time without daring to put my nose out of doors. By the way, about the sale of my works. I have sold my past, present, and future to Marx. I did it, my dear child, in order to put my affairs in order. I am left with fifty thousand (I shall get them finally only in about two years) which will bring me in two thousand roubles a year. Before my agreement with Marx my books brought me in about three thousand five hundred a year, but last year, thanks probably to *The Peasants*, I received eight thousand. Here you have all my business secrets. Do anything you like with them, only don't envy me my ability to make the best of life. However, if by any chance I get to Monte Carlo I shall quite certainly lose about two thousand—a luxury I never dared to dream of till now. But—who knows?—I may win!

" . . . Why am I in Yalta? Why is it so dull here? It is snowing, a blizzard, there is a draught from the windows, the stove is grilling hot, I hate the thought of writing, and I am not writing anything."

I lay on the floor before the huge open file of the paper and, wetting my finger in a plate of water to wash off some of the accumulated dust from the sheet, turned over the pages of every issue, reading the signatures under the sketches.

As Chekhov could remember neither the title of his first story nor the year in which it had appeared, I had to start from the long-distant past. Sometimes I came across stories signed " Ch ", and then I would read them to find whether they had been written by Chekhov.

I asked Chekhov : " Did you ever sign your stories with the letters ' Ch ' ? "

He replied : " I don't remember, my dear child."

My brother-in-law Sergey did not know either.

But the stories signed " Ch " were so bad that I decided not to take any notice of them. In this way I went through the files of two years without finding anything.

My work made me sneeze and sneeze. Every page raised a cloud of dust.

And so I lay writing on the floor while my head was all the time full of Chekhov's letter.

Those were bitter complaints. And Chekhov did not complain so easily, nor had he ever sounded so despondent. That meant that he was having a very bad time indeed.

I remembered a sentence from *About Love* :

" I was unhappy . . ."

Will I never, never bring him anything but grief ?

Chekhov wrote to me often, but in these letters I no longer felt that he wanted me to be near him.

FOURTEEN

IN SPRING I had to go to Moscow. I had incidentally told
Alexey, with whom I was staying, that Chekhov wanted to
buy a house in Moscow for his mother and sister but that he
did not know how to set about it.

" There's nothing easier," said Alexey. " Let's draw up a
list of houses for sale and choose those you think are most
suitable. A friend of mine who is an estate agent will show them
to us. He's a scoundrel, of course, but he won't cheat me. I can
guarantee that. Shall we start ? "

" But you realise that I haven't been authorised to do anything, don't you ? "

" Naturally. Chekhov would never think of that. But if
he wants to buy a house and doesn't know how to set about it,
we must help him."

We both laughed.

" I love buying houses and renting flats," said my brother. " And no one ever suspects that I'm merely enjoying myself and that I couldn't afford to buy a hen-house. They make a fuss of me, run after me, gaze into my eyes. . . . And I inspect everything very carefully. Oh, if you knew what splendid houses there are! Once I nearly bought a palace. . . ."

As I had anyway to go all over the town with the same agent who offered to help me to buy some furniture for my country house, I decided to kill two birds with one stone and at the same time inspect houses which were for sale and which might be suitable for Chekhov. I soon found out that my agent had a knack of buying things for half their price, making full use of circumstances known only to himself, of his business connections and, above all, of his own experience and intelligence.

" I'm doing my best for your brother," he often told me.

" But will you do your best for Chekhov ? "

" You can depend on me. I'll make him a present of a house. We too know something about people. We'll make good our losses by making a bigger profit from another customer."

But on the 23rd of March Chekhov wrote to me : " My money flies away from me like a wild fledgling and in two years I shall have to become a philosopher."

And in April : " If mother and sister still want to buy a house, I shall certainly go and see A. If I buy the house, I shall have nothing left—neither works nor money. I shall have to become a tax assessor."

So I did not buy a house for Chekhov after all.

In Petersburg the business of transcribing Chekhov's stories was drawing to a successful close.

" You are not sending me parcels but bales," Chekhov wrote. " You must have spent at least forty-two roubles on postage alone."

About the middle of April he was already in Moscow. I wrote to tell him that I would be passing through Moscow on the 1st of May, and he replied :

" I shall still be in Moscow on the 1st of May. Could you come and have coffee with me in the morning ? If the children are with you, bring them too. Coffee with rolls and cream ; I'll have some ham, too."

But it was very inconvenient for me to call on the Chekhovs. I had to change trains and there was only about two hours between one train and the other and in that time I had to get breakfast for everybody and try to reserve a compartment. It was hardly worth while going to see Chekhov for a quarter of an hour. I wrote to tell Chekhov about it. However, no sooner had we finished our breakfast than we caught sight of Chekhov who seemed to be looking for us. In his hand he carried a parcel.

" Look what lovely caramels I've got," he said, after exchanging greetings. " Literary ! What do you think ? Shall I ever be honoured in this way ? "

Each caramel was wrapped in a paper with the portraits of Tolstoy, Turgenev, Dostoevsky. . . .

" No Chekhov among them ? Don't worry : it'll soon be there."

Chekhov soon made friends with the children and took little Nina on his knee.

" And why does she look like a schoolmarm ? " he asked.

" Why a schoolmarm ? "

But he fingered Nina's fair curls with such tenderness and looked so lovingly into her large grey eyes that my maternal pride was soothed. Little Nina pressed her head to his shoulder and smiled.

" Children are fond of me," he replied to my surprise that the little girl was not in the least shy of him. " I've a proposal to make to you : this evening they are giving a special performance of *The Seagull* for me. There won't be any audience. Stay till tomorrow. All right ? "

But I could not accept his proposal. It was quite impossible : I would have had to take the children, their French governess and our maid to a hotel, wire my sister in the country and my husband in Petersburg. All that was very complicated and difficult.

" You don't ever agree with me about anything," Chekhov said gloomily. " I should very much like you to see *The Seagull* with me. Can't it be arranged somehow ? "

But however hard we tried to arrange it, we could not think of a way of doing it.

" And have you brought a warm coat ? " Chekhov asked suddenly. " It's dreadfully cold today in spite of its being the 1st of May. I got chilled through and through in my thick winter overcoat while on my way to the station."

" I think you shouldn't have come at all," I said. " You're sure to catch a cold."

" And I think it's sheer madness on your part to travel only in a spring costume. Look here, I'll send a note to Masha* to send you her woollen coat. I can send it straight away. . . . There's still plenty of time."

It took me a lot of trouble to persuade him to give up his idea.

" Well, promise to wire me if you catch a cold and I'll come and attend you. I'm a good doctor, you know. You don't believe I'm a good doctor, do you ? "

* Chekov's sister Mary. (D. M.)

" Come and visit me, but not as a doctor," I said. " Will you ? "

" No," he said quickly and firmly, and immediately changed the subject.

" I gave you a lot of trouble last winter," he said. " Have you really read everything your copyists transcribed ? I felt so sorry for you. And then you've been trying to buy me a house. . . ." He smiled gloomily. " The old woman had no worries," he quoted a Russian proverb, " so she went and bought herself a sucking pig."

The porter came to tell us to take our seats. He took our luggage and went off, followed by the children and their French governess.

Chekhov took my travelling bag and the two boxes of chocolates I was given by the people who had come to see me off in Petersburg. We, too, were about to go when I noticed that his overcoat was unbuttoned.

" That's the way to catch a cold," I remarked.

" That's the way I'm always being reminded that I'm a sick man and no longer good for anything. Must you always remind me of it ? Under all circumstances ? "

" Well, I'm not a sick woman and think of the trouble I had to persuade you not to send to your sister for a warm coat for me. You can think of my catching a cold, but I can't ? "

" So what are we quarrelling about, my dear child ? " Chekhov said and smiled.

" You're not in a good mood today," I observed, adding with a laugh, " although you're wearing new galoshes."

" They aren't new," Chekhov again replied crossly.

We were walking along the platform.

" Do you realise it's now ten years since we first met ? " said Chekhov. " Yes, ten years. We were young then."

" And are we old now ? "

" You—no. I'm worse than an old man. Old men live as and where they like. They enjoy life. My illness binds me hand and foot."

" But you're better now, aren't you ? "

" Don't talk nonsense. You know very well what this improvement in my health is worth. But, you know," he added, suddenly brightening, " I can't help thinking all the same that I can get better, that I can recover my health completely. It's quite possible. Quite possible. Surely, my life isn't finished, is it ? "

Three children's faces were laughing and nodding to us from the window of our compartment.

" Let's go into the carriage," said Chekhov. " You've not only got an awful temper, but you're also a thoughtless and careless woman. Your spring costume makes me angry. How will you travel at night in a horse carriage ? How many miles is it from the station to your country house ? "

The children greeted us as though we had not seen each other for a long time. Chekhov at once took little Nina on his knee again, and my son offered him a book.

" I bought it here from a kiosk. Have you read it ? "

Chekhov took the book and turned over a few pages.

" Oh yes, I've read this book," he said very gravely. " Pushkin's works. It's a good book. You chose well."

Lodya looked very pleased.

" It's poetry. Do you like poetry, Mr. Chekhov ? "

" Yes, I like Pushkin's poetry very much."

" I nearly forgot to give you your last story," I remembered suddenly. " I don't know why it was left behind."

" I can imagine what tripe it is. Have you read it ? "

" No, it isn't tripe. It's a story by Chekhonte. I like Chekhonte's stories very much. He's an excellent writer," I replied, laughing.

" And tonight they're giving a performance of *The Seagull*. Without an audience. Just for me. Oh, what actors! What actors! And I'm very cross with you for refusing to stay. . . ."

The bell rang and Chekhov got up.

I suddenly remembered the parting of Alyokhin and Anna in the compartment of the train just before it moved out of the station. " I embraced her, she clung to me. . . ." I felt my heart beginning to pound suddenly and as though something had hit me on the head.

" But we are not saying good-bye for ever," I tried to console myself. " It's quite possible that he'll come on a visit to me or to Sergey."

I did not see how Chekhov took leave of the children. He did not take leave of me at all, but just walked out into the corridor. I went out after him. He suddenly turned round and looked at me sternly, coldly, almost angrily.

" Even if you were to fall ill, I shouldn't come to see you," he said. " I'm a good doctor, but I should have charged you a very high fee. You wouldn't have been able to afford it. So we shan't see each other again."

He quickly shook my hand and went out.

" Mummy, mummy, come quickly," the children shouted.

The train already began to move slowly. I saw Chekhov's figure sailing past the window, but he did not look back.

I did not know then and I never dreamt that I was seeing him for the last time. . . .

That cold spring night the moon was shining in our garden and the nightingales were singing. There were several of them. When the bird which was singing near our house fell silent, those farther away could be plainly heard, and from the crystal-clear sound of their songs, and the transparent purity of their modulations and trills, the air seemed fresher and more rippling. I stood on the balcony of my room, wrapping myself in a shawl and gazing into the distance where above the tops of the trees the twinkling stars were strewn all over the sky.

I felt cold even in my warm shawl. With hardly a breeze, the air rushed upon me in waves, and the song of the nightingale rang in it like the sound of an ice-cold crystal spring. . . .

FIFTEEN

I WANTED to publish a collection of stories by different hands and devote the proceeds to some charity. I knew a great many writers, some of whom were good friends of mine. I hoped to persuade my brother-in-law Sergey Khudekov to publish it. It seemed to me that both the material and the publication as a whole ought to be excellent and that I would get it all for next to nothing. I had good reason to believe therefore that my work on the collection of stories would bring in a decent amount of money.

First of all I wrote to Chekhov.

He replied that at the moment he had nothing suitable to send me and that, generally, he did not sympathise with my idea.

"If you don't mind my expressing an opinion, then this is what I think : to publish a collection of stories is very slow work, it is very hard work, work that, as a rule, exhausts the editor, but it brings in very little money. This is particularly true of such a collection as you have in mind, i.e., collections of a random character. Please forgive me these unsolicited remarks, but I would have repeated them five, ten, a hundred times, and I would be sincerely glad if I could only persuade you to drop the whole thing. For while you are working on your collection of stories, you could collect thousands of roubles in a different way, not gradually, a spoonful an hour, but immediately, while there is still a keen desire to give. If you must have your collection then publish a small anthology of sayings by the best authors (Shakespeare, Tolstoy, Pushkin, Lermontov etc.) on wounded soldiers, compassion for them, aid, and so on, anything you can find suitable in these authors. This is interesting, and in two or three months the book will be ready and it will sell out quickly. Forgive me for giving you this advice and please don't be indignant with me. By the way, at the present moment no less than fifteen collections are being published. . . ."

He wrote this on 7th February, and on 14th February :

" Dear Lydia Alexeyevna,

" Tomorrow I am leaving for Yalta. If you want to write to me, I shall be very grateful.

" I hope you have made up your mind not to publish your collection. To edit and publish a collection of short stories is a very troublesome and fatiguing business and the profits are very small. In my opinion, it is much better to publish a story in a magazine and send the fee to the Red Cross.

" Forgive me, I am frozen through and through. I have just come back from Tsaritsyn (we travelled in a cab), my hand can hardly write, and, besides, I have to pack. I wish you all the best. Above all, keep cheerful and don't take life too seriously ; very likely it is much more simple. And, anyway, does the life we do not know deserve all the tormenting thoughts which corrode our Russian brains ? I doubt it. I press your hand and thank you very much for your letter.

"Keep well and happy.

"Sincerely, A. Chekhov."

I read the letter hundreds of times. What did this new mood of Chekhov's mean ? "Life is much more simple, it is not worth the tormenting thoughts. . . ." And it seemed to me that he was smiling bitterly, looking back on himself in the past.

BIOGRAPHICAL INDEX OF NAMES

ALBOV, MIKHAIL (1851–1911), writer, 56

AVILOVA, LYDIA (1864–1942), short-story writer, 7, 11, 13–16, 21; meets Chekhov for first time, 13, 29–33; her family life, 35–38; her second meeting with Chekhov, 47–48; first correspondence with Chekhov, 47–48; third meeting, 55–61; Chekhov's declaration of love, 69–70; sends Chekhov engraved watch-chain pendant, 75; their meeting at mask ball, 81–86; first night of *The Seagull*, 16, 94–95; rebuffs Chekhov, 97–99; meeting with Chekhov at Moscow clinic, 101–117; meets Tolstoy, 118; her dream in railway carriage, 119–120; *A Little Joke*, 122; *Forgotten Letters*, 123–124; *About Love*, 25, 124–130; collects Chekhov's early stories, 131–135; last meeting, 25–26, 137–144; her last letters from Chekhov, 145–147.

AVILOVA, MICHAEL, Lydia's husband, a civil servant, 30–32, 35, 36, 44, 52, 59, 80, 103–107, 120, 121

BARANTSEVICH, CASIMIR (1851–1927), writer; began literary work almost at the same time as Chekhov; first met Chekhov in December, 1887; Chekhov thought highly of him both as a writer and a man and in 1900 supported his election to Russian Academy, 56

BURENIN, VIKTOR (1841–1926), novelist, playwright and critic, contributor to reactionary *Novoye Vremya*; met Chekhov for first time in Petersburg in December, 1885; Chekhov was always strongly opposed to his views and only two letters from Chekhov to Burenin are in existence, 68, 74n.

CHEKHOV, ANTON (1860–1904), attitude to Tolstoy, 23, 24; tired of writing, 125; financial position of, 133–134; first serious haemorr-

149

hage, 22, 105–108; hints to writers, 32, 60, 74, 123, 124; house in
Moscow, 25, 137, 138; Korolenko's description of, 11; journey to
Sakhalin, 14; literary output, 13; medical practice and social
work, 8; on family life and the position of women, 51, 52;
relations with Yavorskaya, 19–21; *The Seagull*: autobiographical
elements, 15–18, 82, 81, 85, 90, 91, 94, 95; his flight from Alexandrinsky Theatre, 21, 88–94

CHEKHOV, MARY, b. 1863, Chekhov's sister who helped him with his
literary and social work and whom he made executrix of his
estate, 16, 140

GRIGOROVICH, DIMITRY (1822–1899), well-known novelist, was first
to hail Chekhov as a writer of promise in a letter on 25th March,
1886, in which he expressed his conviction that Chekhov was
destined to write "a number of excellent and really artistic works"
and tried to persuade him to respect his talent and keep it only
"for carefully thought out and polished works written not on the
spur of the moment but in the joyful hours when he was in the
right mood for it;" this letter had a great influence on Chekhov
who talked and wrote a great deal about it; in 1887 Chekhov
dedicated his collection of short stories *At Nightfall* to Grigorovich, thanks to whose recommendation Chekhov was awarded
the Russian Academy Pushkin Prize of 500 roubles in 1889, 12

KHUDEKOV, SERGEY (1837–1913), rich newspaper publisher, editor
of *The Petersburg Gazette* to which Chekhov contributed
regularly from 1885 to 1888; brother-in-law of Lydia Avilova,
11, 30, 32, 33, 39, 41, 132, 145

KNIPPER, OLGA, actress of the Moscow Art Theatre, married
Chekhov on 25th May, 1901, acted leading parts in all Chekhov
plays, 26

KOMMISSARZHEVSKAYA, VERA (1864–1910), famous Russian actress,
played Nina in *The Seagull* at the first performance of the play at
the Alexandrinsky Theatre in Petersburg, later became actress-
manageress of her own theatre, 92

KOROLENKO, VLADIMIR (1851–1921), well-known writer; first met Chekhov in September, 1887; in 1900 both were elected hon. members of the Russian Academy and in 1902 both resigned as a protest against Gorky's expulsion from membership, 11

KRIVENKO, SERGEY, a publicist of the liberal-populist movement, a member of the staff of *The Patriot* in the nineties of the last century, 68

LAZAREV-GRUZINSKY, ALEXANDER (1861–1927), writer, began his literary work almost at the same time as Chekhov whom he first met in 1887; Chekhov took a great interest in his literary progress; frequent visitor to Chekhov's house in Moscow and Melikhovo, 20, 21, 56

LEVKEYEVA, YELISAVETA (1851–1904), famous comic actress of Alexandrinsky Imperial Theatre in Petersburg, 21

LEYKIN, NICOLAI (1841–1906), humorous writer and editor of humorous weekly *Fragments* since 1882 when he first met Chekhov, 13, 50, 55, 56, 60

MARX, A. F., publisher of popular magazine *Niva* to whom Chekhov sold all his past, present and future works for 75,000 roubles and who is reported to have made several hundred thousand roubles profit on his first publication of Chekhov's works in 12 volumes. A letter, signed by a large number of prominent personalities in Russia, was addressed to Marx to ask him to change his contract with Chekhov; the letter was never sent because Chekhov was against it on the ground that he did not think it right to go back on his agreement with Marx as the latter had taken a risk and was therefore entitled to his profits, 132, 133

MIZINOV, LYDIA, a great friend of Mary Chekhov who was a frequent visitor to Chekhov's country house in Melikhovo; later married a well-known producer, 16–19

NEMIROVICH-DANCHENKO, VLADIMIR (1858–1943), novelist and playwright, founded Moscow Art Theatre with Stanislavsky in

1898, a close friend of Chekhov's who was chiefly responsible for putting on his plays at the Moscow Art Theatre, 16, 17, 19, 81, 82

POTAPENKO, IGNATIUS (1856–1926), novelist and playwright, first met Chekhov in Odessa in 1889 and a close friend of his from 1893, accompanied Chekhov to Nice in 1900, 11, 12, 18–21, 56, 58

SHCHEPKINA-KUPERNIK, TATYANA, b. 1874, translator and novelist, a great friend of Chekhov's sister and of Chekhov, 19, 20

SHCHEGLOV (pseudonym of Leontyev), IVAN (1856–1911), novelist and playwright, a close friend of Chekhov's, 22, 24

SUVORIN, ALEXEY (1834–1912), journalist, short-story writer and playwright, ran the theatre of the Literary and Artistic Circle in Petersburg which later became known as Suvorin's Theatre; bought the Petersburg daily *Novoye Vremya* in 1876; began his journalistic work as a liberal but soon became one of the most reactionary publicists in Russia; met Chekhov during the latter's first visit to Petersburg in 1885, and from 1886 to 1893 Chekhov contributed regularly to his paper, altogether publishing 53 stories in it; Chekhov became one of Suvorin's closest friends but was gradually alienated by his extreme conservatism and especially by his attitude towards the Dreyfus case, 14, 20, 24, 40, 61, 70, 82, 86, 90, 97, 98

TOLSTOY, LEO (1828–1910), Chekhov's views on, 23; visit to Chekhov at Moscow clinic, 22–24; meets Lydia Avilova, 117–118

YASSINSKY, HIERONIMUS (1850–1930), writer, 89

YAVORSKAYA, LYDIA (1872–1921), actress, began her stage career in Moscow at Korsh's Theatre, then worked in Suvorin's Theatre, and subsequently became actress-manageress of her own theatre in Petersburg, 19–21, 86, 91